"It may indeed be doubted whether butchers' meat is anywhere a necessary of life. Grain and other vegetables, with the help of milk, cheese, and butter, or oil, where butter is not to be had, afford the most plentiful, the most wholesome, the most nourishing, and the most invigorating diet. Decency nowhere requires than any man should eat butchers' meat."

—Adam Smith
The Wealth of Nations

"I do feel that spiritual progress does demand at some stage that we should cease to kill our fellow creatures for the satisfaction of our bodily wants."

—Gandhi

THE HIGHER TASTE

A Guide to Gourmet Vegetarian Cooking and a Karma-Free Diet

Based on the Teachings of His Divine Grace
A. C. Bhaktivedanta Swami Prabhupāda
Founder-*Ācārya* of
the International Society for Krishna Consciousness

THE BHAKTIVEDANTA BOOK TRUST
Los Angeles • London • Paris • Bombay • Sydney • Hong Kong

International Society for Krishna Consciousness
3764 Watseka Avenue
Los Angeles, CA 90034

Recipes: Bhadrā dāsī (Connie Ball),
Nirākulā dāsī (Noreen Faucett)
Black-and-white drawings: Locana dāsa (chapter
introductions), Guṇamayī dāsī (recipes)
Color illustrations: Parīkṣit dāsa, Muralīdhāra dāsa
Color photography: Nitya-tṛptā dāsī
Cover design: Rohiṇī-priya dāsa, Bhūtātmā dāsa, Locana dāsa

© 1983 Bhaktivedanta Books
Sydney, Australia
All Rights Reserved
Printed in Australia by
The Dominion Press–Hedges & Bell,
Victoria

ISBN: 0-89213-128-4

Dedication

We dedicate this book to our beloved spiritual master and guide, His Divine Grace A. C. Bhaktivedanta Swami Prabhupāda, who brought the transcendental teachings of Lord Kṛṣṇa to the Western world.

—The Editors

Contemporary Vedic Library Series

The Bhaktivedanta Book Trust Contemporary Vedic Library series explores subjects of current interest from the perspective of the timeless knowledge of India's Vedic wisdom.

His Divine Grace A. C. Bhaktivedanta Swami Prabhupāda, founder-*ācārya* (spiritual master) of the International Society for Krishna Consciousness, established the Bhaktivedanta Book Trust in 1970 to present Vedic literatures, as received through the authorized disciplic succession, to the people of the modern age. For the first time in history, through Śrīla Prabhupāda's translations and commentaries, the world's most profound philosophical tradition soon began to have a major impact upon a widespread Western audience. Hundreds of scholars worldwide have reviewed Śrīla Prabhupāda's books, acclaiming his consummate erudition and devotion to the original Sanskrit texts, as well as his unique ability to communicate the most profound and subtle philosophical subjects in a simple and easy-to-understand manner. The Encyclopaedia Britannica reported that his voluminous translations from the original Sanskrit and his lucid commentaries "have astounded literary and academic communities worldwide."

Vedic knowledge has been a source of inner peace, profound wisdom, and spiritual inspiration for millions of people since the dawn of time. The Contemporary Vedic Library editions have been designed to demonstrate practically how this transcendental knowledge, when properly applied, will become a key factor in surmounting the myriad problems facing modern man as we approach the twenty-first century.

Executive Editor
Śrīla Rāmeśvara Swami Mahārāja
Writing and Editorial Board:
Mukunda Goswami (Michael Grant)
Bhūtātmā dāsa (Austin Gordon)
Drutakarmā dāsa (Michael Cremo)

CONTENTS

List of Recipes

═══ Introduction ═══

Influenced by factors ranging from health and economics to ethics and religion, millions of people around the world are turning to a vegetarian diet. In America alone, ten million people now consider themselves vegetarian.

Among those who have renounced meat are many celebrities—film stars Gloria Swanson, William Shatner, Dennis Weaver, Samantha Eggar, Candace Bergen, and Sandy Dennis; recording artists Michael Jackson, Paul and Linda McCartney, George Harrison, John Denver, Johnny Cash, Jeff Beck, Chubby Checker, Graham Nash, David Cassidy, Johnny Rivers, Captain and Tennille, Alice Coltrane, Annie Lennox, Chrissie Hynde, Donovan, Stevie Wonder, and Todd Rundgren; models Brooke Shields and Christine Brinkley. In sports, the list includes Chris Campbell (1981 world wrestling champion), Aaron Pryor (welterweight world boxing champion), Edward Moses (world record holder for 400 meter hurdles), Robert DiCostella (Olympic marathon champion), Anton Innaver (Olympic ski champion), Killer Kowalski (wrestler), and the entire Seibu Lions (Japanese) baseball team (who won the Pacific League championship two years in a row after switching to a vegetarian diet).

The Higher Taste clearly explains the many reasons why people stop eating meat. But beyond that it contains over sixty gourmet vegetarian recipes that are guaranteed to carry you beyond the pleasures of ordinary food into new realms of epicurean delight. If you ever thought that being a vegetarian means eating only limp steamed vegetables and cold salads—you're in for a big surprise. In *The Higher Taste* you'll learn how to prepare complete, nourishing, taste-tempting meals. How about an evening in Italy, with savory minestrone soup, a hearty spaghetti main course complete with veggie-balls in tomato sauce, breaded zucchini sticks, hot ricotta-stuffed calzone, and a Neapolitan cheesecake for dessert? *The Higher Taste* will show you how. You'll also find equally delicious Chinese, Indian, French, Mexican, and Middle Eastern dinners. And best of all, these tested recipes have all been chosen for their simplicity, quickness, and ease of preparation.

Just as important as the ingredients we use in cooking is our consciousness. *The Higher Taste* shows how anyone can turn a daily chore into a blissful, enlightening experience. Preparing *karma*-free vegetarian food is an integral part of the topmost system of *yoga* and meditation described in the timeless teachings of India's Vedic literature. In *Bhagavad-gītā* Lord Kṛṣṇa says, "If one offers Me with love and devotion a leaf, a flower, fruit, or water, I will accept it." One who prepares pure, natural vegetarian food and then offers it to the Supreme will automatically feel an awakening of sublime spiritual pleasure in the heart.

The Supreme Lord is described in the *Vedas* as the reservoir of all pleasure, and to increase His pleasure He expands Himself by His pleasure energy into uncounted millions of living beings who are all meant to share in His enjoyment. We are all part of that eternal pleasure potency, and by the simple act of preparing food for the pleasure of God we can experience transcendental enjoyment. You'll notice that as soon as you taste the food you've offered. As George Harrison said in a recent interview, "When you know someone has begrudgingly cooked something, it doesn't taste as nice as when someone has done it to try and please God, to offer it to Him first. Just that in itself makes all the food taste so much nicer." That's what we mean by "a higher taste."

Along with trying the recipes, be sure to have a look at the opening chapters of *The Higher Taste*. They explain the whole philosophy behind spiritual vegetarianism, and reading them will help you prepare food in the best possible state of mind.

Chapter One reveals how modern medical research has shown links between meat-eating and killer diseases such as cancer and heart disease. Chapter Two exposes the myth of a worldwide food scarcity and explains the economic advantages of a vegetarian diet for society and the individual. In Chapter Three, the ethical foundations of vegetarianism are set forth, focusing on the writings of some of the world's greatest philosophers, authors, and religious leaders, among them Pythagoras, Plato, Leonardo da Vinci, Rousseau, Franklin, Shelley, Tolstoy, Thoreau, Gandhi, and others. The principle of nonviolence, as found in the teachings of Judaism, Christianity, Buddhism, and Hinduism, is also examined. An analysis of how the laws of *karma* and reincarnation are related to vegetarianism forms the basis of Chapter Four. Chapter Five explains in detail the rationale and procedures for offering vegetarian food to the Supreme Lord as part of the *bhakti-yoga* system. In Chapter Six, excerpts from the writings of Śrīla Prabhupāda, India's greatest authority on Vedic culture, provide a concise, highly readable summary of the philosophy underlying the spiritual vegetarian diet outlined in *The Higher Taste*.

An appendix provides an overview of the Kṛṣṇa consciousness movement's varied food-related activities—vegetarian restaurants, self-sufficient farm communities, food-relief programs for the unemployed and underprivileged, and more.

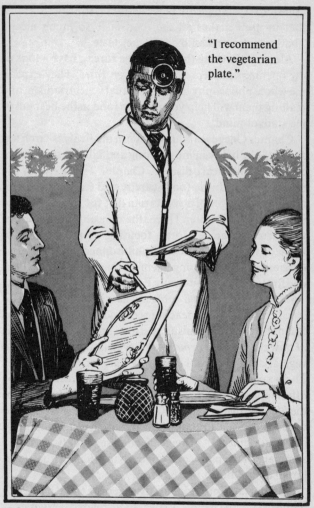

Medical studies link diet to cancer, heart disease, and other killers.

1

Health and a Meatless Diet

The central question about vegetarian diets used to be whether it was healthy to eliminate meat and other animal foods. Now, however, the main question has become whether it is healthier to be a vegetarian than to be a meat eater. The answer to both questions, based on currently available evidence, seems to be yes.

—Jane E. Brody
New York Times News Service

Today, with increasing evidence of diet's critical effect on good health and longevity, more and more people are investigating this question: Is the human body better suited to a vegetarian diet or one that includes meat?

In the search for answers, two areas should be considered—the anatomical structure of the human body, and the physical effects of meat consumption.

Since eating begins with the hands and mouth, what can the anatomy of these bodily parts tell us? Human teeth, like those of the herbivorous creatures, are designed for grinding and chewing vegetable matter. Humans lack the sharp front teeth for tearing flesh that are characteristic of carnivores. Meat-eating animals generally swallow their food without chewing it and therefore do not require molars or a jaw capable of moving sideways. Also, the human hand, with no sharp claws and with its opposable thumb, is better suited to harvesting fruits and vegetables than to killing prey.

1

PHYSIOLOGICAL COMPARISONS

MEAT-EATER	HERBIVORE	MAN
has claws	no claws	no claws
no skin pores, perspires through tongue	perspires through skin pores	perspires through skin pores
sharp front teeth for tearing, no flat molar teeth for grinding	no sharp front teeth has flat rear molars	no sharp front teeth has flat rear molars
intestinal tract 3 times body length so rapidly decaying meat can pass out quickly	intestinal tract 10–12 times body length	intestinal tract 12 times body length
strong hydrochloric acid in stomach to digest meat	stomach acid 20 times less strong than meat-eaters	stomach acid 20 times less strong than meat-eaters

Digesting Meat

Once within the stomach, meat requires digestive juices high in hydrochloric acid. The stomachs of humans and herbivores produce acid less than one-twentieth the strength of that found in carnivores.

Another crucial difference between the meat-eater and the vegetarian is found in the intestinal tract, where the food is further digested and nutrients are passed into the blood. A piece of meat is just part of a corpse, and its putrefaction creates poisonous wastes within the body. Therefore meat must be quickly eliminated. For this purpose, carnivores possess alimentary canals only three times the length of their bodies. Since man, like other non-flesh-eating animals, has an alimentary canal twelve times his body length, rapidly decaying flesh is retained for a much longer time, producing a number of undesirable toxic effects.

One body organ adversely affected by these toxins is the kidney. This vital organ, which extracts waste from the blood, is strained by the overload of poisons introduced by meat consumption. Even moderate meat-eaters demand three times more work from their kidneys than do vegetarians. The kidneys of a young person may be able to cope with this stress, but as one grows older the risk of kidney disease and failure greatly increases.

Heart Disease

The inability of the human body to deal with excessive animal fats in the diet is another indication of the unnaturalness of meat-eating. Carnivorous animals can metabolize almost unlimited amounts of cholesterol and fats without any adverse effects. In experiments with dogs, up to one half pound of butterfat was added to their daily diet over a period of two years, producing absolutely no change in their serum cholesterol level.

On the other hand, the vegetarian species have a very limited ability to deal with any level of cholesterol or saturated fats beyond the amount required by the body. When over a period of many years an excess is consumed, fatty deposits (plaque) accumulate on the inner walls of the arteries, producing a condition known as arteriosclerosis, hardening of the arteries. Because the plaque deposits constrict the flow of blood to the heart, the potential for heart attacks, strokes, and blood clots is tremendously increased.

As early as 1961, the *Journal of the American Medical Association* stated that ninety to ninety-seven percent of heart disease, the cause of more than one half of the deaths in the United States, could be prevented by a vegetarian diet.[1] These findings are supported by an American Heart Association report that states, "In well-documented population studies using standard methods of diet and coronary disease assessment . . . evidence suggests that a high-saturated-fat diet is an essential factor for a high incidence of coronary heart disease."[2] The National Academy of Sciences also reported recently that the high serum cholesterol level found in most Americans is a major factor in the coronary heart disease "epidemic" in the United States.[3]

Cancer

Further evidence of the unsuitability of the human intestinal tract for digestion of flesh is the relationship, established by numerous studies, between colon cancer and meat-eating.[4] One reason for the incidence of cancer is the high-fat, low-fiber content of the meat-centered diet. This results in a slow transit time through the colon, allowing toxic wastes to do their damage. States Dr. Sharon Fleming of the Department of Nutritional Sciences at the University of California at Berkeley, "Dietary fiber appears to aid in reducing . . . colon and rectal cancer."[5] Moreover, while being digested, meat is known to generate steroid metabolites possessing carcinogenic (cancer-producing) properties.

As research continues, evidence linking meat-eating to other forms of cancer is building up at an alarming rate. The National Academy of Sciences reported in 1983 that "people may be able to prevent many common cancers by eating less fatty meats and more vegetables and grains."[6] And in his *Notes on the Causation of Cancer,* Rollo Russell writes, "I have found of twenty-five nations eating flesh largely, nineteen had a high cancer rate and only one had a low rate, and that of thirty-five nations eating little or no flesh, none had a high rate."[7]

Some of the most shocking results in cancer research have come from exploration of the effects of nitrosamines. Nitrosamines are formed when secondary amines, prevalent in beer, wine, tea, and tobacco, for example, react with chemical preservatives in meat. The Food and Drug Administration has labeled nitrosamines "one of the most formidable and versatile groups of carcinogens yet discovered, and their role . . . in the etiology of human cancer has caused growing apprehension among experts." Dr. William Lijinsky of Oak Ridge National Laboratory conducted experiments in which nitrosamines were fed to test animals. Within six months he found malignant tumors in one hundred percent of the animals. "The cancers," he said, "are all over the place; in the brain, lungs, pancreas, stomach, liver, adrenals, and intestines. The animals are a bloody mess."[8]

Dangerous Chemicals in Meat

Numerous other potentially hazardous chemicals, of which consumers are generally unaware, are present in meat and meat products. In their book *Poisons in Your Body,* Gary and Steven Null give us an inside look at the latest gimmicks used in the corporate-owned animal factories. "The animals are kept alive and fattened by the continuous administration of tranquilizers, hormones, antibiotics, and 2,700 other drugs," they write. "The process starts even before birth and continues long after death. Although these drugs will still be present in the meat when you eat it, the law does not require that they be listed on the package."

One of these chemicals is diethylstilbestrol (DES), a growth hormone that has been used in the U.S. for the last twenty years despite studies that have shown it to be carcinogenic. Banned as a serious health hazard in thirty-two countries, it continues to be used by the U.S. meat industry, possibly because the FDA estimates it saves meat producers more than $500 million annually.

Another popular growth stimulant is arsenic. In 1972 this well-known poison was found by the U.S. Department of Agriculture (USDA) to exceed the legal limit in fifteen percent of the nation's poultry.[9]

Sodium nitrate and sodium nitrite, chemicals used as preservatives to slow down putrefaction in cured meat and meat products, including ham, bacon, bologna, salami, frankfurters, and fish, also endanger health. These chemicals give meat its bright-red appearance by reacting with pigments in the blood and muscle. Without them, the natural gray-brown color of dead meat would turn off many prospective consumers.

Unfortunately, these chemicals do not distinguish between the blood of a corpse and the blood of a living human, and many persons accidentally subjected to excessive amounts have died of poisoning. Even smaller quantities can prove hazardous, especially for young children or babies, and therefore the United Nations' joint FAO/WHO Expert Committee on Food Additives warned, "Nitrate should on no account be added to baby food." A. J. Lehman of the FDA pointed out that "only a small margin of safety exists between the amount of nitrate that is safe and that which may be dangerous."

Because of the filthy, overcrowded conditions forced upon animals by the livestock industry, vast amounts of antibiotics must be used. But such rampant use of antibiotics naturally creates antibiotic-resistant bacteria that are passed on to those who eat the meat. The FDA estimates that penicillin and tetracycline save the meat industry $1.9 billion a year, giving them sufficient reason to overlook the potential health hazards.

The trauma of being slaughtered also adds "pain poisons" (such as powerful stimulants) into the meat. These join with uneliminated wastes in the animal's blood, such as urea and uric acid, to further contaminate the flesh the consumers eat.

Diseases in Meat

In addition to dangerous chemicals, meat often carries diseases from the animals themselves. Crammed together in unclean conditions, force-fed, and inhumanely treated, animals destined for slaughter contract many more diseases than they ordinarily would. Meat inspectors attempt to filter out unacceptable meats, but because of pressures from the industry and lack of sufficient time for examination, much of what passes is far less wholesome than the meat purchaser realizes.

A 1972 USDA report lists carcasses that passed inspection after the diseased parts were removed. Examples included nearly 100,000 cows with eye cancer and

3,596,302 cases of abscessed liver. The government also permits the sale of chickens with airsacculitis, a pneumonialike disease that causes pus-laden mucus to collect in the lungs. In order to meet federal standards, the chicken's chest cavities are cleaned out with air-suction guns. But during this process diseased air sacs burst and pus seeps into the meat.

The USDA has even been found to be lax in enforcing its own low standards. In its capacity of overseeing federal regulatory agencies, the U.S. General Acccounting Office cited the USDA for failure to correct various violations by slaughterhouses. Carcasses contaminated with rodent feces, cockroaches, and rust were found in meat-packing companies such as Swift, Armour, and Carnation.[10] Some inspectors rationalize the laxity, explaining that if regulations were enforced, no meat-packers would remain open for business.

Nutrition Without Meat

Many times the mention of vegetarianism elicits the predictable reaction, "What about protein?" To this the vegetarian might well reply, "What about the elephant? And the bull? And the rhinoceros?" The ideas that meat has a monopoly on protein and that large amounts of protein are required for energy and strength are both myths. While it is being digested, most protein breaks down into its constituent amino acids, which are reconverted and used by the body for growth and tissue replacement. Of these twenty-two amino acids, all but eight can be synthesized by the body itself, and these eight "essential amino acids" exist in abundance in nonflesh foods. Dairy products, grains, beans, and nuts are all concentrated sources of protein. Cheese, peanuts, and lentils, for instance, contain more protein per ounce than hamburger, pork, or porterhouse steak. A study by Dr. Fred Stare of Harvard and Dr. Mervyn Hardinge of Loma Linda University made extensive comparisons between the protein intake of vegetarians and flesh-eaters. They concluded that "each group exceeded twice its requirement for every essential amino acid and surpassed this amount by large margins for most of them."

For many Americans, protein makes up more than twenty percent of their diet, nearly twice the quantity recommended by the World Health Organization. Although inadequate amounts of protein will cause loss of strength, excess protein cannot be utilized by the body; rather, it is converted into nitrogenous wastes that burden the kidneys. The primary energy source for the body is carbohydrates. Only as a last resort is the body's protein utilized for energy production. Too much protein intake actually reduces the body's energy capacity. In a series of comparative endurance tests conducted by Dr. Irving Fisher of Yale, vegetarians performed twice as well as meat-eaters. By reducing the nonvegetarians' protein consumption by twenty percent, Dr. Fisher found their efficiency increased by thirty-three percent. Numerous other studies have shown that a proper vegetarian diet provides more nutritional energy than meat. Furthermore, a study by Dr. J. Iotekyo and V. Kipani at Brussels University showed that vegetarians were able to perform physical tests two to three times longer than meat-eaters before exhaustion and were fully recovered from fatigue in one fifth the time needed by the meat-eaters.

References

1. "Diet and Stress in Vascular Disease," *Journal of the American Medical Association,* June 3, 1961, p. 806.

2. "Diet and Coronary Heart Disease," a statement developed by the Committee on Nutrition and authorized for release by the Central Committee for Medical and Community Programs of the American Heart Association, 1973.

3. "Diet and Coronary Heart Disease," *Journal of the American Medical Association,* vol. 222, no. 13, (Dec. 25, 1972), p. 1647.

4. Michael J. Hill, M.D., "Metabolic Epidemiolgy of Dietary Factors in Large Bowel Cancer," *Cancer Research,* vol. 35, no. 11, part 2 (Nov., 1975), pp. 3398–3402; Bandaru S. Reddy, Ph.D. and Ernest L. Wynder, M.D., "Large-Bowel Carcinogenesis: Fecal Constituents of Population with Diverse Incidence Rates of Colon Cancer," *Journal of the National Cancer Institute,* vol. 50, 1973, pp. 1437–41.

5. Dr. Sharon Fleming, personal correspondence, Feb. 26, 1981.

6. *Los Angeles Herald Examiner.*

7. Quoted from *Cancer and Other Diseases from Meat Consumption,* Blanche Leonardo, Ph.D., 1979, p. 12.

8. Statement of Dr. William Lijinsky, U.S. House of Representatives' hearing "Regulation of Food Additives and Medicated Animal Foods," March 1971, p. 132.

9. "Arsenic in Chicken Liver to Be Reviewed by Agency," *Wall Street Journal,* Jan. 13, 1972.

10. Jean Snyder, "What You'd Better Know About the Meat You Eat," *Today's Health,* vol. 19, Dec. 1971, pp. 38–39.

BUMPER CORN CROP, YUTON, ILLINOIS

APPALACHIA

In 1983 the U.S. government's surplus food stockpile included 1 million tons of rice, 18 million bushels of wheat, 431 million bushels of corn, 33 million pounds of honey, 715 million pounds of butter, 1.8 billion pounds of dried milk, and 1.1 billion pounds of cheese.

2

The Hidden Cost of Meat
The Myth of Scarcity

In his 1975 bestseller, The Eco-Spasm Report, *futurist Alvin Toffler, author of* Future Shock *and* The Third Wave, *suggested a positive hope for the world's food crisis. He anticipated "the sudden rise of a religious movement in the West that restricts the eating of beef and thereby saves billions of tons of grain and provides a nourishing diet for the world as a whole."*

Solving the Hunger Problem

Food expert Francis Moore Lappé, author of the best-selling *Diet for a Small Planet,* said in a recent television interview that we should look at a piece of steak as a Cadillac. "What I mean," she explained, "is that we in America are hooked on gas-guzzling automobiles because of the illusion of cheap petroleum. Likewise, we got hooked on a grain-fed, meat-centered diet because of the illusion of cheap grain."

According to information compiled by the United States Department of Agriculture, over ninety percent of all the grain produced in America is used for feeding livestock—cows, pigs, lambs, and chickens—that wind up on dinner tables. Yet the process of using grain to produce meat is incredibly wasteful. For example, information from the USDA's Economic Research Service shows that we get back only one pound of beef for every sixteen pounds of grain.

In his book *Proteins: Their Chemistry and Politics,* Dr. Aaron Altshul notes that in terms of calorie units per acre, a diet of grains, vegetables, and beans will support twenty times more people than a diet of meat. As it stands now, about half the harvested acreage in America is used to feed animals. If the earth's arable land were used primarily for the production of vegetarian foods, the planet could easily support a human population of twenty billion and more.

Facts such as these have led food experts to point out that the world hunger problem is largely illusory. The myth of "overpopulation" should not be used by advocates of abortion to justify the killing of more than fifty million unborn children worldwide each year. Even now, we are already producing enough food for everyone on the planet, but unfortunately it is being allocated inefficiently. In a report submitted to the United Nations World Food Conference (Rome, 1974), Rene Dumont, an agricultural economist at France's National Agricultural Institute, made this judgment: "The overconsumption of meat by the rich means hunger for the poor. This wasteful agriculture must be changed—by the suppression of feedlots where beef are fattened on grains, and even a massive reduction of beef cattle."

Living Cows Are an Economic Asset

It is quite clear that a living cow yields society more food than a dead one—in the form of a continuing supply of milk, cheese, butter, yogurt and other high-protein foods. In 1971, Stewart Odend'hal of the University of Missouri conducted a detailed study of cows in Bengal and found that far from depriving humans of food, they ate only inedible remains of harvested crops (rice hulls, tops of sugarcane, etc.) and grass. "Basically," he said, "the cattle convert items of little direct human value into products of immediate utility." This should put to rest the myth that people are starving in India because they will not kill their cows. Interestingly enough, India recently seems to have surmounted its food problems, which have always had more to do with occasional severe drought or political upheaval than with sacred cows. A panel of experts at the Agency for International Development, in a statement cited in the *Congressional Record* for December 2, 1980, concluded, "India produces enough to feed all its people."

If allowed to live, cows produce high quality, protein-rich foods in amounts that stagger the imagination. In America, there is a deliberate attempt to limit dairy production; nevertheless, Representative Sam Gibbons of Florida recently reported to Congress that the U.S. government was being forced to stockpile "mountains of butter, cheese, and nonfat dried milk." He told his colleagues, "We currently own about 440 million pounds of butter, 545 million pounds of cheese, and about 765 million pounds of nonfat dried milk." The supply grows by about 45 million pounds each week. In fact, the 10 million cows in American provide so much milk that the government periodically releases millions of pounds of dairy products for free distribution to the poor and hungry. It's abundantly clear that cows (living ones) are one of mankind's most valuable food resources.

Movements to save seals, dolphins, and whales from slaughter are flourishing—so why shouldn't there be a movement to save the cow? From the economic standpoint alone, it would seem to be a sound idea—unless you happen to be part of the meat industry, which is increasingly worried about the growth of vegetarianism. In June 1977, a major trade magazine, *Farm Journal,* printed an editorial entitled, "Who Will Defend the Good Name of Beef?" The magazine urged the nation's beef-cattle raisers to chip in $40 million to finance publicity to keep beef consumption and prices sky high.

You're Paying More than You Think for Meat

The meat industry is a powerful economic and political force, and besides spending millions of its own dollars to promote meat-eating, it has also managed to grab an unfair share of our tax dollars. Practically speaking, the meat production process is so wasteful and costly that the industry needs subsidies in order to survive. Most people are unaware of how heavily national governments support the meat industry by outright grants, favorable loan guarantees, and so forth. In 1977, for example, the USDA bought an extra $100 million of surplus beef for school lunch programs. That same year, the governments of Western Europe spent almost a half-billion dollars purchasing the farmers' overproduction of meat and spent additional millions for the cost of storing it.

More tax dollars go down the drain in the form of the millions of dollars the U.S. government spends each year to maintain a nationwide network of inspectors to monitor the little-publicized problem of animal diseases. When diseased animals are destroyed, the government pays the owners an indemnity. For instance, in 1978 the American government paid out $50 million of its citizens' tax money in indemnities for the control of brucellosis, a flulike disease that afflicts cattle and other animals. Under another program, the U.S. government guarantees loans up to $350,000 for meat producers. Other farmers receive guarantees only up to $20,000. A *New York Times* editorial called this subsidy bill "outrageous," characterizing it as "a scandalous steal out of the public treasury." Also, despite much evidence from government health agencies showing the link between meat-eating and cancer and heart disease, the USDA continues to spend millions promoting meat consumption through its publications and school lunch programs.

Environmental Damage

Another price we pay for meat-eating is degradation of the environment. The United States Agricultural Research Service calls the heavily contaminated runoff and sewage from America's thousands of slaughterhouses and feedlots a major source of pollution of the nation's rivers and streams. It is fast becoming apparent that the fresh water resources of this planet are not only becoming polluted but also depleted, and the meat industry is particularly wasteful. In their book *Population, Resources, and Environment,* Paul and Anne Ehrlich found that to grow one pound of wheat requires only 60 pounds of water, whereas production of a pound of meat requires anywhere from 2,500 to 6,000 pounds of water. And in 1973 the *New York Post* uncovered this shocking misuse of a valuable national resource—one large chicken slaughtering plant in America was found to be using 100 million gallons of water daily! This same volume would supply a city of 25,000 people.

Social Conflict

The wasteful process of meat production, which requires far larger acreages of land than vegetable agriculture, has been a source of economic conflict in human society for thousands of years. A study published in *Plant*

Foods for Human Nutrition reveals that an acre of grains produces five times more protein than an acre of pasture set aside for meat production. An acre of beans or peas produces ten times more, and an acre of spinach twenty-eight times more protein. Economic facts like these were

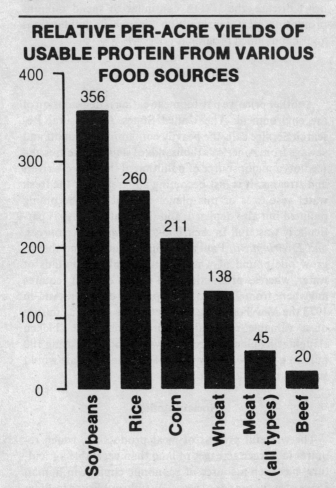

RELATIVE PER-ACRE YIELDS OF USABLE PROTEIN FROM VARIOUS FOOD SOURCES

known to the ancient Greeks. In Plato's *Republic* the great Greek philosopher Socrates recommended a vegetarian diet because it would allow a country to make the most intelligent use of its agricultural resources. He warned that if people began eating animals, there would be need for more pasturing land. "And the country which was enough to support the original inhabitants will be too small now, and not enough?" he asked of Glaucon, who replied that this was indeed true. "And so we shall go to war, Glaucon, shall we not?" To which Glaucon replied, "Most certainly."

It is interesting to note that meat-eating played a role in many of the wars during the age of European colonial expansion. The spice trade with India and other countries of the East was an object of great contention. Europeans subsisted on a diet of meat preserved with salt. In order to disguise and vary the monotonous and unpleasant taste of their food, they eagerly purchased vast quantities of spices. So huge were the fortunes to be made in the spice trade that governments and merchants did not hesitate to use arms to secure sources.

In the present era there is still the possibility of mass conflict based on food. Back in August 1974, the Central Intelligence Agency (CIA) published a report warning that in the near future there may not be enough food for the world's population "unless the affluent nations make a quick and drastic cut in their consumption of grain-fed animals."

Saving Money with a Vegetarian Diet

But now let's turn from the world geopolitical situation, and get right down to our own pocketbooks. Although not widely known, grains, beans, and milk products are an excellent source of high-quality protein.

Pound for pound many vegetarian foods are better sources of this essential nutrient than meat. A 100-gram portion of meat contains only 20 grams of protein. (Another fact to consider: meat is more than 50% water by weight.) In comparison, a 100-gram portion of cheese or lentils yields 25 grams of protein, while 100 grams of soybeans yields 34 grams of protein. But although meat provides less protein, it costs much more. A spot check of supermarkets in Los Angeles in August 1983 showed sirloin steak costing $3.89 a pound, while staple ingredients for delicious vegetarian meals averaged less than 50 cents a pound. An eight-ounce container of cottage cheese costing 59 cents provides 60% of the minimum daily requirement of protein. Becoming a vegetarian could potentially save an individual shopper at least several hundred dollars each year, thousands of dollars over the course of a lifetime. The savings to America's consumers as a whole would amount to billions of dollars annually. Considering all this, it's hard to see how anyone could afford not to become a vegetarian.

"I do feel that spiritual progress does demand at some stage that we should cease to kill our fellow creatures for the satisfaction of our bodily wants."

—Gandhi

3

"Do Unto Others . . ."

I have no doubt that it is a part of the destiny of the human race, in its gradual improvement, to leave off eating animals.

—Thoreau

I do feel that spiritual progress does demand at some stage that we should cease to kill our fellow creatures for the satisfaction of our bodily wants.

—Gandhi

Each year about 134 million mammals and 3 billion birds are killed for food in America. But few people make any conscious connection between this slaughter and the meat products that appear on their tables. A case in point: in television commercials a clown called Ronald McDonald tells kiddies that hamburgers grow in "hamburger patches." The truth is not so pleasant—commercial slaughterhouses are like visions of hell. Screaming animals are stunned by hammer blows, electric shock, or concussion guns. They are then hoisted into the air by their feet and moved through the factories of death on mechanized conveyor systems. Often still alive, their throats are sliced and their flesh is cut off. Describing his reaction to a visit to a slaughterhouse, champion tennis player Peter Burwash wrote in his book *A Vegetarian Primer,* "I'm no shrinking violet. I played hockey until half of my teeth were knocked down my throat. And I'm extremely competitive on a tennis court. . . . But that experience at the slaughterhouse overwhelmed me. When I walked out of there, I knew I would never again harm an animal! I knew all the physiological, economic, and ecological arguments supporting vegetarianism, but it was firsthand experience of man's cruelty to animals that laid the real groundwork for my commitment to vegetarianism."

Ancient Greece and Rome

Ethical considerations have always attracted many of the world's greatest personalities to adopt a vegetarian diet. Pythagoras, famous for his contributions to geometry and mathematics, said, "Oh, my fellow men, do not defile your bodies with sinful foods. We have corn, we have apples bending down the branches with their weight, and grapes swelling on the vines. There are sweet-flavored herbs, and vegetables which can be cooked and softened over the fire, nor are you denied milk or thyme-scented honey. The earth affords a lavish supply of riches, of innocent foods, and offers you banquets that involve no bloodshed or slaughter; only beasts satisfy their hunger with flesh, and not even all of those, because horses, cattle, and sheep live on grass." The biographer Diogenes tells us that Pythagoras ate bread and honey in the morning and raw vegetables at night. He would also pay fishermen to throw their catch back into the sea.

In an essay titled "On Eating Flesh," the Roman author Plutarch wrote: "Can you really ask what reason Pythagoras had for abstinence from flesh? For my part I rather wonder both by what accident and in what state of mind the first man touched his mouth to gore and brought his lips to the flesh of a dead creature, set forth tables of dead, stale bodies, and ventured to call food and nourishment the parts that had a little before bellowed and cried, moved and lived. How could eyes endure the slaughter when throats were slit and hides flayed and limbs torn from limb? How could his nose endure the stench? How was it that the pollution did not turn away his taste, which made contact with sores of others and sucked juices and serums from mortal wounds? It is certainly not lions or wolves that we eat out of self-defense; on the contrary, we ignore these and slaughter harmless, tame creatures without stings or teeth to harm us. For the sake of a little flesh we deprive them of sun, of light, of the duration of life to which they are entitled by birth and being."

He then delivered this challenge to flesh-eaters: "If you declare that you are naturally designed for such a diet, then first kill for yourself what you want to eat. Do it, however, only through your own resources, unaided by cleaver or cudgel or any kind of ax."

Da Vinci, Rousseau, Franklin . . .

The great Renaissance painter, inventor, sculptor, and poet Leonardo da Vinci epitomized the ethical approach to vegetarianism. He wrote, "He who does not value life does not deserve it." He considered the bodies of meat-eaters to be "burial places," graveyards for the animals they eat. His notebooks are full of passages that show his compassion for living creatures. He lamented, "Endless numbers of these animals shall have their little children taken from them, ripped open, and barbarously slaughtered."

French philosopher Jean Jacques Rousseau was an advocate of natural order. He observed that the meat-eating animals are generally more cruel and violent than herbivores. He therefore reasoned that a vegetarian diet would produce a more compassionate person. He even advised that butchers not be allowed to testify in court or sit on juries.

In *The Wealth of Nations* economist Adam Smith proclaimed the advantages of a vegetarian diet. "It may indeed be doubted whether butchers' meat is anywhere a necessary of life. Grain and other vegetables, with the help of milk, cheese, and butter, or oil, where butter is not to be had, afford the most plentiful, the most wholesome, the most nourishing, and the most invigorating diet. Decency nowhere requires than any man should eat butchers' meat." Similar considerations motivated Benjamin Franklin, who became a vegetarian at age sixteen. Franklin noted "greater progress, from that greater clearness of head and quicker apprehension." In his autobiographical writings, he called flesh-eating "unprovoked murder."

The poet Shelley was a committed vegetarian. In his essay "A Vindication of Natural Diet," he wrote, "Let the advocate of animal food force himself to a decisive experiment on its fitness, and as Plutarch recommends, tear a living lamb with his teeth and, plunging his head into its vitals, slake his thirst with the steaming blood. . . . then, and then only, would he be consistent." Shelley's interest in vegetarianism began when he was a student at Oxford, and he and his wife, Harriet, took up the diet soon after their marriage. In a letter dated March 14, 1812, his wife wrote to a friend, "We have foresworn meat and adopted the Pythagorean system." Shelley, in his poem *Queen Mab*, described a Utopian world where men do not kill animals for food.

. . . no longer now
He slays the lamb that looks him in the face,
And horribly devours his mangled flesh,
Which, still avenging Nature's broken law,
Kindled all putrid humors in his frame,
All evil passions, and all vain belief,
Hatred, despair, and loathing in his mind,
The germs of misery, death, disease and crime.

The Russian author Leo Tolstoy became a vegetarian in 1885. Giving up the sport of hunting, he advocated "vegetarian pacifism" and was against killing even the smallest living things, such as the ants. He felt there was a natural progression of violence that led inevitably to war in human society. In his essay "The First Step," Tolstoy wrote that flesh-eating is "simply immoral, as it involves the performance of an act which is contrary to moral feeling—killing." By killing, Tolstoy believed, "man suppresses in himself, unnecessarily, the highest spiritual capacity—that of sympathy and pity towards living creatures like himself—and by violating his own feelings becomes cruel."

Composer Richard Wagner believed that all life was sacred. He saw vegetarianism as "nature's diet," which could save mankind from violent tendencies and help us return to the "long-lost Paradise."

At various times in his life, Henry David Thoreau was a vegetarian. Although his own practice of vegetarianism was spotty at best, he recognized its virtues. In *Walden* he wrote, "Is it not a reproach that man is a carnivorous animal? True, he can and does live, in a great measure, by preying on other animals; but this is a miserable way—as any one who will go to snaring rabbits, or slaughtering lambs, may learn—and he will be regarded as a benefactor of his race who shall teach man to confine himself to a more innocent and wholesome diet. Whatever my own practice may be, I have no doubt that it is a part of the destiny of the human race, in its gradual improvement, to leave off eating animals, as surely as the savage tribes have left off eating each other when they came in contact with the more civilized."

The Twentieth Century

It goes without saying that the great twentieth-century apostle of nonviolence Mohandas Gandhi was a vegetarian. His parents, being devout Hindus, never gave him meat, fish, or eggs. Under British rule, however, there was a great attack on the age-old principles of Indian culture. Under such pressures, many Indians began to adopt the meat-eating habits of the West. Even Gandhi fell victim to the advice of some schoolfriends, who urged him to eat meat because it would increase his strength and courage. But he later resumed a vegetarian diet and wrote, "It is necessary to correct the error that vegetarianism has made us weak in mind, or passive or inert in action. I do not regard flesh-food as necessary at any stage." He wrote five books on vegetarianism. His own daily diet included wheat sprouts, almond paste, greens, lemons, and honey. He founded Tolstoy Farm, a community based on vegetarian principles. In his *Moral Basis of Vegetarianism* Gandhi wrote, "I hold flesh-food to be unsuited to our species. We err in copying the lower animal world if we are superior to it." He felt that ethical principles are a stronger support for lifelong commitment to a vegetarian diet than reasons of health. "I do feel," he stated, "that spiritual progress does demand at some stage that we should cease to kill our fellow creatures for the satisfaction of our bodily wants."

Playwright George Bernard Shaw first tried to become a vegetarian at age twenty-five. "It was Shelley who first opened my eyes to the savagery of my diet," he wrote in his autobiography. Shaw's doctors warned that the diet would kill him. When an old man, he was asked why he didn't go back and show them what good it had done him. He replied, "I would, but they all passed away years ago." Once someone asked him how it was that he looked so youthful. "I don't," Shaw retorted. "I look my age. It is the other people who look older than they are. What can you expect from people who eat corpses?" On the connection between flesh-eating and violence in human society, Shaw wrote:

> We pray on Sundays that we may have light
> To guide our footsteps on the path we tread;
> We are sick of war, we don't want to fight,
> And yet we gorge ourselves upon the dead.

H. G. Wells wrote about vegetarianism in his vision of a future world, *A Modern Utopia*. "In all the round world of Utopia there is no meat. There used to be. But now we cannot stand the thought of slaughterhouses. And, in a population that is all educated, and at about the same level of physical refinement, it is practically impossible to find anyone who will hew a dead ox or pig. . . . I can still remember as a boy the rejoicings over the closing of the last slaughterhouse."

Nobel-prize–winning author Isaac Bashevis Singer became a vegetarian in 1962, at age fifty-eight. He said, "Naturally I am sorry now that I waited so long, but it is better later than never." He finds vegetarianism quite compatible with his mystical variety of Judaism. "We are all God's creatures—that we pray to God for mercy and justice while we continue to eat the flesh of animals that are slaughtered on our account is not consistent." Although he appreciates the health aspect of vegetarianism, he states very clearly that the ethical consideration is primary. "Even if eating flesh was actually shown to be good for you, I would certainly still not eat it."

Singer has little patience with intellectual rationalizations for meat-eating. "Various philosophers and religious leaders tried to convince their disciples and followers that animals are nothing more than machines without a soul, without feelings. However, anyone who has ever lived with an animal—be it a dog, a bird, or even a mouse—knows that this theory is a brazen lie, invented to justify cruelty."

Vegetarianism and Religion

Avoidance of meat has been a part of religious practice in nearly all faiths. Some Egyptian priests were vegetarians, avoiding meat in order to help them maintain vows of celibacy. They also avoided eggs, which they called "liquid flesh."

Although the Old Testament, the foundation of Judaism, contains some prescriptions for meat-eating, it is clear that the ideal situation is vegetarianism. In Genesis (1:29) we find God Himself proclaiming: "Behold, I have given you every herb bearing seed, which is upon the face of all the earth, and every tree, in that which is the fruit of a tree yielding seed; to you it shall be for meat." In the beginning of creation as described in the Bible, it seems that not even the animals ate flesh. In Genesis (1:30) God says, "And to every beast of the earth, and to every fowl of the air, and to every thing that creepeth upon the earth, wherein there is life, I have given every green herb for meat; and it was so." Genesis (9:4) also directly forbids meat-eating: "But flesh with the life thereof, which is the blood thereof, shall ye not eat. And surely your blood of your lives will I require; at the hand of every beast will I require it."

In later books of the Bible, major prophets also condemn meat-eating. Isaiah (1:5) states, "Saith the Lord: I am full of the burnt offerings of rams, and the fat of fed beasts; and I delight not in the blood of bullocks, or of lambs, or of he-goats. When ye spread forth your hands, I will hide Mine eyes from you: yea, when ye make many prayers, I will not hear, for your hands are full of blood." According to Isaiah (66:3), the killing of cows is particularly abhorrent: "He that killeth an ox is as if he slew a man."

In the Bible we also find the story of Daniel, who while imprisoned in Babylon refused to eat the meat offered by his jailers, preferring instead simple vegetarian food.

Major stumbling blocks for many Christians are the belief that Christ ate meat and the many references to meat in the New Testament. But close study of the original Greek manuscripts shows that the vast majority of the words translated as "meat" are *trophe, brome*, and other words that simply mean "food" or "eating" in the broadest sense. For example, in the Gospel of St. Luke (8:55) we read that Jesus raised a woman from the dead and "commanded to give her meat." The original Greek word translated as "meat" is *phago*, which means only "to eat." So what Christ actually said was, "Let her eat." The Greek word for meat is *kreas* ("flesh"), and it is never used in connection with Christ. Nowhere in the New Testament is there any direct reference to Jesus eating meat. This is in line with Isaiah's famous prophecy about Jesus's appearance: "Behold, a virgin shall conceive, and bear a son, and shall call his name Immanuel. Butter and honey shall he eat, that he may know to refuse the evil and choose the good."

Clement of Alexandria, an early Church father, recommended a fleshless diet, citing the example of the apostle Matthew, who "partook of seeds, and nuts, and vegetables, without flesh." St. Jerome, another leader of the early Christian Church, who gave the authorized Latin version of the Bible still in use today, wrote, "The preparation of vegetables, fruit, and pulse is easy, and does not require expensive cooks." He felt such a diet was the best for a life devoted to the pursuit of wisdom. St. John Chrysostom considered meat-eating to be a cruel and unnatural habit for Christians. "We imitate but the ways of wolves, but the ways of leopards, or rather we are even worse than these. For to them nature has assigned that they should be thus fed, but us God hath honored with speech and a sense of equity, and we are become worse than the wild beasts." St. Benedict, who founded the Benedictine Order in A.D. 529, stipulated vegetable foods as the staple for his monks. The Trappist order uniformly prohibited meat, eggs, and other flesh foods from its founding in the seventeenth century. The regulations were relaxed by the Vatican Councils of the 1960s, but most of the Trappists still follow the original teachings. Remarkably enough, however, many Trappist monasteries raise cattle for slaughter to support themselves financially.

The Seventh Day Adventist Church strongly recommends vegetarianism for its members. Although little known to the general public, the huge American breakfast cereals industry got its start at an Adventist health resort run by Dr. John H. Kellogg. Dr. Kellogg was constantly devising new varieties of vegetarian breakfast foods for the wealthy patients of his Battle Creek Sanitorium. One of his inventions was cornflakes, which he later marketed nationwide. Over the course of time, he gradually separated his business from the Seventh Day Adventist Church and formed the company that still bears his name.

The largest concentration of vegetarians in the world is found in India, the homeland of Buddhism and Hinduism. Buddhism began as a reaction to widespread animal slaughter that was being carried out through perversion of religious rituals. Buddha put an end to these practices by propounding his doctrine of *ahiṁsā,* or nonviolence.

Indian Philosophy and Nonviolence

The Vedic scriptures of India, which predate Buddhism, also stress nonviolence as the ethical foundation of vegetarianism. The *Manu-saṁhitā,* the ancient Indian code of law, states, "Meat can never be obtained without injury to living creatures, and injury to sentient beings is detrimental to the attainment of heavenly bliss; let him therefore shun the use of meat." In another section, the *Manu-saṁhitā* warns, "Having well considered the disgusting origin of flesh and the cruelty of fettering and slaying of corporeal beings, let him entirely abstain from eating flesh."

In recent years the Hare Kṛṣṇa movement has introduced these ethical considerations around the world. Śrīla Prabhupāda, the movement's founder-*ācārya* (spiritual master), once stated, "In the *Manu-saṁhitā* the concept of a life for a life is sanctioned, and it is actually observed throughout the world. Similarly, there are other laws which state that one cannot even kill an ant without being responsible. Since we cannot create, we have no right to kill any living entity, and therefore man-made laws that distinguish between killing a man and killing an animal are imperfect. . . . According to the laws of God, killing an animal is as punishable as killing a man. Those who draw distinctions between the two are concocting their own laws. Even in the Ten Commandments it is prescribed, 'Thou shalt not kill.' This is a perfect law, but by discriminating and speculating men distort it. 'I shall not kill man, but I shall kill animals.' In this way people cheat themselves and inflict suffering on themselves and others."

Emphasizing the Vedic conception of the unity of all life, Śrīla Prabhupāda then stated, "Everyone is God's creature, although in different bodies or dresses. God is considered the one supreme father. A father may have many children, and some may be intelligent and others not very intelligent, but if an intelligent son tells his father, 'My brother is not very intelligent; let me kill him,' will the father agree? . . . Similarly, if God is the supreme father, why should He sanction the killing of animals who are also His sons?"

Is there a connection between the violence human beings inflict upon each other in war and the violence humans inflict upon the animals they slaughter for meat? According to the law of *karma*, the answer is yes.

4

Karma and Reincarnation

In human society, if one kills a man he has to be hanged
[or punished]. That is the law of the state. Because of
ignorance people do not perceive that there is a complete
state controlled by the Supreme Lord. Every living crea-
ture is the son of the Supreme Lord, and He does not
tolerate even an ant's being killed. One has to pay for it.
                                               —Śrīla Prabhupāda

Capital punishment is the state's ultimate act of repri-
sal, and no sacrifice surpasses offering one's life for the
sake of others. But although we seemingly attach great
value to life, each year in America hundreds of millions of
defenseless animals are butchered. This wholesale slaughter of animals is not necessary to prevent us from starving.
Moreover, it is economically extravagant and ethically
reprehensible. Most seriously, however, animal killing
violates of the universal law of *karma,* which is similar to
the modern scientific principle of action and reaction.

Scientists clearly understand how the physical law of
action and reaction ("for every action there is an equal
and opposite reaction") applies to material objects, but

37

most are unaware of the more subtle law of action and
reaction in the realm of consciousness. Nevertheless, we
do have a kind of instinctive awareness that somehow we
all create our own happiness and distress. This realization
dawns upon us when in response to some mishap we
reflect, "Well, maybe I had that coming to me."

In fact, we sometimes find people jokingly attributing
unfortunate occurrences in their lives to "bad *karma*."
But the law of *karma,* like any other law, is ultimately no
joking matter. It operates impartially and unerringly,
awarding us exactly what we deserve. Specifically, the law
of *karma* insures that those who cause violence and suffering to other living beings must themselves experience
equivalent violence and suffering—immediately or in the
future.

Karma, as many in the West now know, is intimately
related with the principle of reincarnation. In India's
greatest spiritual classic, *Bhagavad-gītā,* Lord Kṛṣṇa describes the soul as the source of consciousness and the
active principle that animates the body of every living
being. This vital force, which is of the same spiritual
quality in all beings, is distinct from and superior to the
matter comprising the temporary material form. At the
time of death, the indestructible soul transmigrates into
another physical body, just as one changes clothing. All
living beings (not just a few select individuals) undergo
this process of reincarnation, lifetime after lifetime. The
Bhagavad-gītā states, "As a person puts on new garments,
giving up old ones, similarly, the soul accepts new material bodies, giving up the old and useless ones."

The Journey of the Soul

The *Vedas* explain that the soul, known as the *ātmā,*
may inhabit any of 8,400,000 general species of material

bodies. The physical forms vary in complexity, beginning with the primitive microbes and amoebas, continuing on through the aquatic, plant, insect, reptile, bird, and animal species, and culminating in human beings and demigods. In consequence of its own desires to enjoy matter, the *ātmā* continually journeys through these various bodies, on an endless voyage of births and deaths.

The action of the mind is the prime force compelling the living entity to transmigrate from one body to another. The *Gītā* explains, "Whatever state of being one remembers when he quits his body, that state of being he will attain without fail." Our minds are constantly recording all of our thoughts and desires, and the totality of these memories floods our consciousness in the last moments of life. The nature of our thoughts at this critical juncture propels us into the appropriate physical body. Thus the body we now occupy is an accurate physical projection of our state of mind at the time of our last death.

The *Bhagavad-gītā* explains, "The living entity, thus taking another gross body, obtains a certain type of eye, ear, tongue, nose, and sense of touch, which are grouped around the mind. He thus enjoys a particular set of sense objects."

According to the *Vedas,* a soul in a form lower than human automatically evolves to the next-higher species, ultimately arriving at the human form. But because the human being possesses freedom to choose between matter and spirit, there is a chance that the soul will descend again into the lower species. The laws of *karma* are so arranged that if a human lives and dies with the animalistic mentality of a creature such as a dog, then in the next life he will be able to fulfill his doglike desires through the senses and organs of a dog. This is certainly an unfortunate occurrence, but such a fate is a definite possibility for a person immersed in ignorance. The *Gītā* declares, "When he dies in the mode of ignorance, he takes birth in the animal kingdom."

So the soul in the body of an animal may once have inhabited a human form and vice versa. Although a soul may successively occupy plant, animal, and human bodies, its intrinsic nature remains the same. Because the soul is pure spiritual energy, it cannot be altered in any way by matter. *Bhagavad-gītā* explains that the soul is "immutable and unchangeable." It is only the bodily covering, with its particular combination of mind and senses, that temporarily restricts or releases the conscious energy of the soul.

The Equality of All Living Things

The basic and transcendental equality of all conscious entities is not an abstract notion but is obvious to everyday sense perception—if only we look beyond the superficial differences in the varieties of material bodies. Anyone who has ever had a pet or visited the zoo has experienced that animals behave much like humans as they search for food, protect their young, play, sleep, and fight. The outstanding difference is that their intelligence and emotions are less developed, but this distinction is insufficient to discount the far more numerous and significant similarities in thinking, feeling, and willing that clearly point toward the universal equality of the consciousness within all bodies.

In nonhuman species, the living being is stringently controlled by his natural instincts. He is deprived of freedom of choice in eating, sleeping, mating, and defending, being compelled by bodily demands to follow rigid behavioral patterns. For this reason, the *ātmā* dwelling within forms of life lower than human is not responsible for its actions and thus does not generate new *karma*. A similar principle operates within our everyday experience—a dog chasing a cat across the roadway is immune from any traffic citations. Animals are not expected to understand or obey a sophisticated set of laws. On the other hand, in both the social order and the universal order, a human being is obliged to be informed and obedient.

Therefore, when a human unnecessarily takes the life of another entity, especially under conditions of great pain and suffering, this act of overt aggression produces a severe karmic reaction. And, if year after year millions of animals are mercilessly butchered in huge, mechanized slaughterhouses, the accumulated negative *karma* produced by all those participating is almost unfathomable.

In his *Bhagavad-gītā* commentary, His Divine Grace A. C. Bhaktivedanta Swami Prabhupāda sternly warns about the karmic danger of animal slaughter. "In human society, if one kills a man he has to be hanged. That is the law of the state. Because of ignorance people do not perceive that there is a complete state controlled by the Supreme Lord. Every living creature is the son of the Supreme Lord, and He does not tolerate even an ant's being killed. One has to pay for it."

"Do Unto Others . . . "

This same instruction is present in all religious teachings. The Bible emphatically states, "Thou shall not kill," and Lord Jesus Christ, who always displayed deep compassion for all living beings, stated, "Do unto others as you would have them do unto you." Lord Buddha also taught the principle of *ahiṁsā*, nonviolence, specifically to protect innocent creatures from being slaughtered.

People who find that personally killing an animal is too gruesome tend to believe that merely eating flesh does not implicate them in violence. But this opinion is short-sighted and unsupported by any valid spiritual authority. According to the law of *karma,* all those who are connected to the killing of an animal are liable—the person who gives permission for the killing, the person who kills, the person who helps, the person who purchases the meat, the person who cooks the flesh, and the person who eats it. (These six guilty parties are enumerated in the *Manu-saṁhitā,* ancient India's book of civic and religious codes.) In a court of law all those who conspire in a murder are considered responsible, especially the party who purchases the assassin's services.

Psychological and emotional growth are essential to a progressive life, and all our thoughts and actions influence our character development. The Bible explains, "As you sow, so shall you reap." And the subtle laws of *karma* inform us that negative personality traits such as hostility, cruelty, depression, arrogance, apathy, insensitivity, anxiety, and envy are the psychological harvest of those who directly or indirectly make killing a regular feature in their life. When someone adopts a vegetarian diet, it is much easier for him to remain peaceful, happy, productive, and concerned for the welfare of others. As the brilliant physicist Albert Einstein said, "The vegetarian manner of living, by it's purely physical effect on the human temperament, would most beneficially influence the lot of mankind." But when human consciousness is polluted by the effects of the negative *karma* resulting from destructive and injurious actions, its good qualities become covered.

The Cause of Violence

At present, despite impressive progress in science and technology, the world is faced with a crisis of unremitting violence in the shape of wars, terrorism, murder, vandalism, child abuse, and abortion. More than 140 wars have been fought since the United Nations was formed in 1945, and in America alone, 20,000 people are murdered each year. With social and political solutions conspicuously failing, perhaps it's time to analyze the problem from a different perspective—the law of *karma*. The callous and brutal slaughter of countless helpless animals must be considered as a powerful causative factor in this wave of uncheckable violence.

In his purports to the *Śrīmad-Bhāgavatam*, Śrīla Prabhupāda has pointed out how the widespread violence among humans is a karmic reaction to animal slaughter. "In this age the propensity for mercy is almost nil. Consequently there is always fighting and wars between men and nations. Men do not understand that because they unrestrictedly kill so many animals, they must also be slaughtered like animals in big wars. This is very much evident in the Western countries. In the West, slaughterhouses are maintained without restriction, and therefore every fifth or tenth year there is a big war in which countless people are slaughtered even more cruelly than the animals. Sometimes during war, soldiers keep their enemies in concentration camps and kill them in very cruel ways. These are reactions brought about by unrestricted animal-killing in the slaughterhouse and by hunters in the forest."

The question is sometimes raised that if the *ātmā* (soul) is completely transcendental to the material body, why should killing, if great pain is avoided, be considered wrongful violence? Even the *Bhagavad-gītā* states, "For the soul there is neither birth nor death. He is not slain when the body is slain." In his *Śrīmad-Bhāgavatam* purports, Śrīla Prabhupāda addresses this question. "All living entities have to fulfill a certain duration for being encaged in a particular type of material body. They have to finish the duration allotted in a particular body before being promoted or evolved to another body. Killing an animal or any other living being simply places an impediment in the way of his completing his term of imprisonment in a certain body. One should therefore not kill bodies for one's sense gratification, for this will implicate one in sinful activity." In short, killing an animal interrupts its progressive evolution through the species.

We can also appreciate the unjustness of animal-killing by seeing that the body is a dwelling place for the *ātmā* residing within. An individual unexpectedly driven out of his comfortable home suffers great inconvenience and distress. Such merciless and unjustified action is undoubtedly criminal. Furthermore, in order to receive his next material body, the living being must suffer extended prebirth tribulations. For the human being this involves months of being tightly packed in the darkness of the womb, where one is constantly disturbed by infections, acid fluids burning the skin, jarring motions, and discomforts resulting from the eating and drinking habits of the mother.

Is Killing Vegetables Wrong?

Another common metaphysical question is, "If all living entities are spiritually equal, then why is it acceptable to eat grains, vegetables, etc., and not meat? Aren't vegetarians guilty of killing vegetables?" In response, it may be pointed out that vegetarian foods such as fruits, nuts, milk, and grains do not require any killing. But even in those cases where a plant's life is taken, the pain involved is much less than when an animal is slaughtered, because the plant's nervous system is less developed. Clearly there is a vast difference between pulling a carrot out of the ground and killing a lamb. But still, one must undoubtedly suffer karmic reactions even for killing plants.

For this reason, Lord Kṛṣṇa explains in *Bhagavad-gītā* that not only should man eat only vegetarian foods, but he should also offer these eatables to Him. If we follow this process of sacrifice, the Supreme Lord, Kṛṣṇa, protects us from any karmic reactions resulting from the killing of plants. Otherwise, according to the law of *karma,* we are personally responsible. The *Gītā* states, "The devotees of the Lord are released from all sins because they eat food that is offered first for sacrifice. Others, who prepare food for personal sense enjoyment, verily eat only sin."

Śrīla Prabhupāda elaborates on this principle of spiritual vegetarianism. "Human beings are provided with food grains, vegetables, fruits, and milk by the grace of the Lord, but it is the duty of human beings to acknowledge the mercy of the Lord. As a matter of gratitude, they should feel obliged to the Lord for their supply of foodstuff, and they must first offer Him food in sacrifice and then partake of the remnants." By eating such sanctified food—*prasādam*—one is protected from karmic reactions and advances spiritually.

Anyone can transform ordinary eating into a spiritual experience by offering vegetarian foods to Lord Kṛṣṇa.

5

Beyond Vegetarianism

*If one offers Me with love and devotion a leaf, a flower,
fruit, or water, I will accept it.*
>   —*Bhagavad-gītā* (9.26)

Beyond concerns of health, psychology, economics,
ethics, and even *karma*, vegetarianism has a higher, spiritual dimension that can help us develop our natural appreciation and love for God.

Walking through a supermarket, people may forget a
very basic fact of nature—it's not man but God who
makes food. There's something mystical about the way
food grows. You put a tiny seed in the ground, it sprouts,
and by the mysterious life force within it a food factory
arises—a tomato plant producing dozens of tasty red
tomatoes, an apple tree producing bushels of sweet apples. No team of scientists anywhere has yet invented
anything as amazing as the simplest green creation of
God.

But rather than admit the existence of a superior intelligence, scientists mislead the public with their theories of
chemical evolution. Without substantial evidence, they
proclaim that life comes from chemicals. Yet they cannot
utilize those chemicals to make a seed that will grow into a
shaft of wheat that will produce more seeds that will

sprout into hundreds of more shafts of wheat.

Once we admit that life comes only from life, it's entirely reasonable to suppose that all life originates from a common living source, the one Supreme Lord, known to the Muslims as Allah, to the Jews as Yahweh, to the Christians as Jehovah, and to the followers of the *Vedas* as Kṛṣṇa.

So at very least we should offer our food to God out of gratitude. Every religion has such a process of thanksgiving. But the spiritual path outlined in the Vedic scriptures of India is unique in that the offering of food to the Lord is part of a highly developed form of *yoga* that helps one develop one's personal loving relationship with God. This is called *bhakti-yoga*.

Originally, each soul has a direct relationship with God in the spiritual world, and according to the *Vedas* the main purpose of life is to revive this lost relationship. The *Śrīmad-Bhāgavatam*, a classic Sanskrit work known as the ripened fruit of the tree of Vedic knowledge, states, "The human form of life affords one a chance to return home, back to Godhead. Therefore every living entity, especially in the human form of life, must engage in devotional service."

Devotional service, or *bhakti-yoga,* is the highest form of *yoga*. In *Bhagavad-gītā,* after discussing various kinds of *yoga,* Lord Kṛṣṇa, the master of all *yoga,* declares, "Of all *yogīs,* one who always abides in Me with great faith, worshiping Me in transcendental loving service [*bhakti*], is most intimately united with Me in *yoga* and is highest of all." Lord Kṛṣṇa further states, "One can understand the Supreme Personality as He is only by devotional service. And when one is in full consciousness of the Supreme Lord by such devotion, he can enter into the kingdom of God."

The Yoga of Eating

Summarizing the process of *bhakti-yoga,* the *yoga* of devotion, the Lord says, "All that you do, *all that you eat,* all that you offer and give away, as well as all austerities that you may perform, should be done as an offering unto Me." So offering food is an integral part of the *bhakti-yoga* system.

The Lord also describes the types of offerings that He will accept. "If one offers Me with love and devotion a leaf, a flower, fruit, or water, I will accept it." Kṛṣṇa specifically does not include meat, fish, or eggs in this list; therefore a devotee does not offer them to Him. Out of love, the devotee offers Kṛṣṇa only the purest and choicest foods—and these certainly do not include the weeks-old rotting corpses of slaughtered animals or the potential embryos of chickens.

In most religious systems people ask God to feed them ("Give us this day our daily bread"), but in Kṛṣṇa consciousness the devotee offers food to God as an expression of love for Him. Even in ordinary dealings, somebody will prepare a meal as a sign of love and affection. It isn't only the meal itself that is appreciated, but the love and consideration that goes into it. In the same way, the process of offering food to God is intended to help us increase our love and devotion toward Him. Of course, it is very difficult to love someone we have never seen. Fortunately, the Vedic scriptures, unique in all the world, describe God's personal features in great detail.

The Vedic conception of God is not vague. In the scriptures of other major religions God is briefly mentioned as the Supreme Father, but surprisingly little information is given about His personality. Christ spoke of himself as being the son of God, and Muhammad was His prophet; but what of God Himself? He appears only indirectly—as a voice from heaven, a burning bush, and so on.

However, once we admit that God has created us, then we cannot reasonably deny that He Himself possesses all the attributes of personhood—a distinct form and appearance, and all the powers and abilities of various senses and organs. It is illogical to suppose that the creature of God can in any way surpass his creator. If we possess distinct forms and personalities, and God were not to possess them, then we would be superior to Him in that respect. So just as we are persons, God is also a person—the Supreme Person, with an infinitely powerful spiritual form, but nevertheless a person. After all, it is said that we are created in the image and likeness of God.

Using their imaginations, Western artists have generally depicted God as a powerfully built old man with a beard. But the Vedic scriptures of India give direct descriptions of God's personality—information found nowhere else. First of all, God is eternally youthful, and He possesses wonderful spiritual qualities that attract the minds of liberated souls. He is the supreme artist, the supreme musician. He speaks wonderfully and manifests unlimited intelligence, humor, and genius. Moreover, He displays incomparable transcendental pastimes with His eternal associates. There is no end to the descriptions of the attractive features of the Personality of Godhead found in the *Vedas*. Therefore He is called Kṛṣṇa, or "all-attractive." When we understand God's personal identity, it becomes much easier to meditate upon Him, especially when offering Him food.

Because Kṛṣṇa is supremely powerful and completely spiritual, anything that comes in contact with Him also becomes completely pure and spiritual. Even in the realm of physical nature certain things have the ability to purify various substances. For instance, the sun, with its powerful rays, can distill fresh, pure water from a lake contaminated with pollutants. If a material object like the sun can act in this way, then we can only imagine the purifying potency of the Supreme Personality of Godhead, who has effortlessly created millions of suns.

Spiritual Food

By His immense transcendental energies, Kṛṣṇa can actually convert matter to spirit. If we place an iron rod in fire, before long the iron rod becomes red hot and takes on all the essential qualities of fire. In the same way, the material substance of food that is offered to Kṛṣṇa becomes completely spiritualized. Such food is called *prasādam*, a Sanskrit word meaning "the mercy of the Lord."

Eating *prasādam* is a fundamental practice of *bhakti-yoga*. In other forms of *yoga*, one is required to restrain the senses, but the *bhakti-yogi* is free to use his senses in a variety of pleasing spiritual activities. For instance, he can use his tongue to taste the delicious foods offered to Lord Kṛṣṇa. By such activities, the senses gradually become spiritualized and automatically become attracted to divine pleasures that far surpass any material experience.

The Vedic scriptures contain many descriptions of *prasādam* and its effects. Lord Caitanya, an incarnation of the Supreme Lord who appeared in India five hundred years ago, said of *prasādam*, "Everyone has tasted these material substances before. However, in these ingredients there are extraordinary tastes and uncommon fragrances. Just taste them and see the difference in the experience. Apart from the taste, even the fragrance pleases the mind and makes one forget any other sweetness besides its own. Therefore it is to be understood that the spiritual nectar of

Kṛṣṇa's lips has touched these ordinary ingredients and transferred to them all their spiritual qualities."

Eating only food offered to Kṛṣṇa is the ultimate perfection of a vegetarian diet. After all, even many animals such as pigeons and monkeys are vegetarian, so becoming a vegetarian is in itself not the greatest accomplishment. The *Vedas* inform us that the purpose of human life is reawakening the soul's original relationship with God, and only when we go beyond vegetarianism to *prasādam* can our eating be helpful in achieving this goal.

How to Prepare and Offer *Prasādam*

Our consciousness of the higher purpose of vegetarianism begins as we walk down the supermarket aisles selecting the foods we will offer to Kṛṣṇa. In *Bhagavad-gītā,* Lord Kṛṣṇa states that all foods can be classified according to the three modes of material nature—goodness, passion, and ignorance. Milk products, sugar, vegetables, fruits, nuts, and grains are foods in the mode of goodness and may be offered to Kṛṣṇa. As a general rule, foods in the modes of passion and ignorance are not offerable to Kṛṣṇa, who says in the *Gītā* that such eatables "cause pain, distress, and disease" and are "putrid, decomposed, and unclean." As may be guessed, meat, fish, and eggs are foods in the lower modes. But there are also a few vegetarian items that are classified in the lower modes—garlic and onions, for example. They should not be offered to Kṛṣṇa. (Hing, sometimes called asafetida, is an acceptable substitute for them in cooking and is available in most Oriental or Indian specialty shops.) Coffees and teas that contain caffein are also considered to be in the lower modes. If you like beverages of this sort, purchase caffein-free coffees and herbal teas.

In shopping, you should be aware that you may find meat, fish, and egg products mixed in with other foods, so be sure to study labels carefully. For instance, some brands of yogurt and sour cream contain gelatin, which is prepared from the horns, hooves, and bones of slaughtered animals. Make sure any cheese you purchase is rennetless, because rennet is an enzyme extracted from the stomach tissues of calves.

You should also avoid foods precooked by people who are not devotees of Kṛṣṇa. According to the subtle laws of nature, the cook acts upon the food not only physically, but mentally as well. Food thus becomes an agency for subtle influences on our consciousness. To give another example of this principle, a painting is not simply a collection of strokes on a canvas. It is also an expression of the artist's state of mind, and this mental content is absorbed by the person who looks at the painting. Similarly, if we eat foods cooked by people devoid of spiritual consciousness—employees working in a factory somewhere—then we are sure to absorb a dose of materialistic mental energies. As far as possible, use only fresh, natural ingredients.

In preparing food, cleanliness is the most important principle. Nothing impure should be offered to God, so keep your kitchen work-area very clean. Always wash your hands thoroughly before preparing food. While preparing food, do not taste it. This is part of meditating that you are cooking the meal not simply for yourself but for the pleasure of Kṛṣṇa, who should be the first to enjoy it. When the meal is prepared, you are ready to offer it. Arrange portions of the food on diningware kept especially for this purpose. (No one else should eat from these dishes.) The very simplest form of offering is to simply pray, "My dear Lord Kṛṣṇa, please accept this food."

Remember that the real purpose of this is to show your devotion and gratitude to the Lord; the actual food you are offering is secondary. Without this devotional feeling, the offering will not be accepted. God is complete in Himself; He has no need of anything. Our offering is simply a means for us to show our love and gratitude toward Him. Following the offering one should chant for a few minutes the Hare Kṛṣṇa *mantra*: Hare Kṛṣṇa, Hare Kṛṣṇa, Kṛṣṇa Kṛṣṇa, Hare Hare/ Hare Rāma, Hare Rāma, Rāma Rāma, Hare Hare. Then the *prasādam* may be served. Try to appreciate the spiritual quality of *prasādam* by remembering how it frees one from the effects of *karma*. But above all, enjoy it.

Eventually you may wish to make a more formal offering according to the procedures established by the Hare Kṛṣṇa movement for persons who desire to practice Kṛṣṇa consciousness in their own homes. Briefly, this involves setting up a simple altar with pictures of Lord Kṛṣṇa and the spiritual master, learning some simple Sanskrit *mantras,* and so forth. If you would like to learn how to do this, please contact the Kṛṣṇa temple nearest you or write to the secretary for ISKCON Educational Services (3764 Watseka Avenue, Los Angeles, CA 90034).

Other Principles of *Bhakti-yoga*

Of course, offering *prasādam* is only part of the process of *bhakti-yoga*. In order to further purify your consciousness and spiritualize your senses, you can practice other items of devotional service. The first of these is the regular chanting of the Hare Kṛṣṇa *mantra*—Hare Kṛṣṇa, Hare Kṛṣṇa, Kṛṣṇa Kṛṣṇa, Hare Hare/ Hare Rāma, Hare Rāma, Rāma Rāma, Hare Hare. The *Kalisantaraṇa Upaniṣad* states, "These sixteen names composed of thirty-two syllables are the only means to counteract the evil effects of Kali-yuga [the present age of quarrel and hypocrisy]. In all the *Vedas* it is seen that to cross the ocean of nescience there is no alternative to the chanting of the holy name." The Hare Kṛṣṇa *mantra* may be chanted either congregationally, sometimes to the accompaniment of musical instruments, or quietly as a private meditation. For private meditation, the recommended procedure is to chant the Hare Kṛṣṇa *mantra* on beads especially made for this purpose. For further information, see the Contemporary Vedic Library Series book *Chant and Be Happy,* which fully explains the process of Hare Kṛṣṇa *mantra* meditation.

To improve the quality of your spiritual life, you should also avoid the use of intoxicants—drugs, alcohol, and cigarettes, as well as soft drinks, coffee, and tea if they contain caffein. Using these substances unnecessarily clouds the mind, which is already clouded with all kinds of material concepts of life. The *Vedas* also recommend that a person attempting to advance in spiritual life have nothing to do with gambling, for it invariably puts one in anxiety and fuels greed, envy, and anger. Another activity that increases material desires and blocks the growth of spiritual awareness is illicit sex. The regulations of *bhakti-yoga* do, however, allow sex within the context of marriage.

By following the principles mentioned above, one can always experience increasing spiritual pleasure as a tangible part of one's life. In particular, one's offerings of food become more pleasing to Kṛṣṇa. God does not require the food we offer; rather, He appreciates the degree of purity and devotion in our hearts as we offer it.

Eventually, one should take initiation from a bona fide spiritual master, without whose instruction and guidance it is not possible to attain the perfection of Kṛṣṇa consciousness. In *Bhagavad-gītā* Lord Kṛṣṇa says, "Just try to learn the truth by approaching a spiritual master. Inquire from him submissively and render service unto him. The self-realized soul can impart knowledge unto you because he has seen the truth."

The original spiritual master of the Kṛṣṇa consciousness movement in the Western world is His Divine Grace A. C. Bhaktivedanta Swami Prabhupāda. Śrīla Prabhupāda is a member of the authorized chain of disciplic succession reaching back through time to Lord Kṛṣṇa Himself, the supreme spiritual master. Shortly before he departed this world in 1977, Śrīla Prabhupāda appointed a number of his most advanced disciples as spiritual masters to carry on the line of succession, and since that time other spiritual masters have been designated.

Śrīla Prabhupāda, renowned as India's greatest cultural and spiritual ambassador to the world, personally instructed his disciples in the art of preparing and distributing *prasādam*. Furthermore, in his books and public lectures, he extensively explained the Vedic philosophy underlying the practice of offering food to Kṛṣṇa. "We should remember then that it is not vegetarianism which is important," Śrīla Prabhupāda once said. "The important thing is that we simply have to try to learn how to love Kṛṣṇa. Love begins with give and take. We give something to our lover, he gives something to us, and in this way love develops." Anyone can enter into this loving transaction by offering vegetarian foods to Kṛṣṇa and accepting the remnants as *prasādam*.

His Divine Grace
A. C. Bhaktivedanta Swami Prabhupāda
Founder-Ācārya of the International Society for Krishṇa Consciousness

6

A Higher Taste

(*Excerpts from the writings of
His Divine Grace
A. C. Bhaktivedanta Swami Prabhupāda*)

The Myth of Scarcity

With the good will of the Supreme Personality of Godhead there can be enough fruits, grains, and other foodstuffs produced so that all the people in the world could not finish them, even if they ate ten times their capacity. In this material world there is actually no scarcity of anything but Kṛṣṇa consciousness. If people become Kṛṣṇa conscious, by the transcendental will of the Supreme Personality of Godhead there will be enough foodstuffs produced so that people will have no economic problems at all. One can very easily understand this fact. The production of fruits and flowers depends not upon our will but the supreme will of the Personality of Godhead. If He is pleased, He can supply enough fruits, flowers, etc., but if people are atheistic and godless, nature, by His will, restricts the supply of food.

Caitanya-caritāmṛta (*Ādi* 9.38)

God Is a Vegetarian

Mr. Faill: Is it necessary to follow certain eating habits to practice spiritual life?

Śrīla Prabhupāda: Yes, the whole process is meant to purify us, and eating is part of that purification. I think you have a saying, "You are what you eat," and that's a fact. Our bodily constitution and mental atmosphere are determined according to how and what we eat. Therefore the *śāstras* [scriptures] recommend that to become Kṛṣṇa conscious, you should eat remnants of food left by Kṛṣṇa [*kṛṣṇa-prasādam*]. If a tuberculosis patient eats something and you eat the remnants, you will be infected with tuberculosis. Similarly, if you eat *kṛṣṇa-prasādam*, then you will be infected with Kṛṣṇa consciousness. Thus our process is that we don't eat anything immediately. First we offer the food to Kṛṣṇa, then we eat it. This helps us advance in Kṛṣṇa consciousness.

Mr. Faill: You are all vegetarians?

Śrīla Prabhupāda: Yes, because Kṛṣṇa is a vegetarian. Kṛṣṇa can eat anything because He is God, but in the *Bhagavad-gītā* [9.26] He says, "If one offers Me with love and devotion a leaf, a flower, a fruit, or water, I will accept it." He never says, "Give Me meat and wine."

Science of Self-Realization (p. 185)

There Is No Scarcity

If we throw a bag of grain into the street, pigeons may come and eat four or five small grains and then go away. They will not take more than they can eat, and having eaten they go freely on their way. But if we were to put many bags of flour on the sidewalk and invite people to come and get them, one man would take ten or twenty bags and another would take fifteen or thirty bags and so on. But those who do not have the means to carry so much away will not be able to take more than a bag or two. Thus the distribution will be uneven. This is called advancement of civilization; we are even lacking in the knowledge which the pigeons, dogs, and cats have. Everything belongs to the Supreme Lord, and we can accept whatever we need, but not more. That is knowledge. By the Lord's arrangement the world is so made that there is no scarcity of anything. Everything is sufficient, provided that we know how to distribute it. However, the deplorable condition today is that one is taking more than he needs while another is starving.

Rāja-vidyā (p. 91)

"Thou Shalt Not Kill"

Śrīla Prabhupāda: We have to accept all the injunctions of the scripture as they are given, not only those that suit us. If you do not follow the first order, "Thou shalt not kill," then where is the question of love of God?

Visitor: Christians take this commandment to be applicable to human beings, not to animals.

Śrīla Prabhupāda: That would mean that Christ was not intelligent enough to use the right word: *murder*. There is *killing*, and there is *murder*. *Murder* refers to human beings. Do you think Jesus was not intelligent enough to use the right word—*murder*—instead of the word *killing*? *Killing* means any kind of killing, and especially animal killing. If Jesus had meant simply the killing of humans, he would have used the word *murder*. . . If you want to interpret these words, that is something else. We understand the direct meaning. "Thou shalt not kill" means "The Christians should not kill."

Father Emmanuel: Isn't the eating of plants also killing?

Śrīla Prabhupāda: The Vaiṣṇava philosophy teaches that we should not even kill plants unnecessarily. In the *Bhagavad-gītā* [9.26] Kṛṣṇa says: "If someone offers Me with love and devotion a leaf, a flower, a fruit, or a little water, I will accept it." We offer Kṛṣṇa only the kind of food He demands, and then we eat the remnants. If offering vegetarian food to Kṛṣṇa were sinful, then it would be Kṛṣṇa's sin, not ours. But God is *apāpa-viddha*—sinful reactions are not applicable to Him. . . . Eating food first offered to the Lord is also something like a soldier's killing during wartime. In a war, when the commander orders a man to attack, the obedient soldier who kills the enemy will get a medal. But if the same soldier kills someone on his own, he will be punished. Similarly, when we eat only *prasādam* [the remnants of food offered to Kṛṣṇa], we do not commit any sin. This is confirmed in the *Bhagavad-gītā* [3.13]: "The devotees of the Lord are released from all kinds of sins because they eat food that is first offered for sacrifice. Others, who prepare food for personal sense enjoyment, verily eat only sin."

Father Emmanuel: Kṛṣṇa cannot give permission to eat animals?

Śrīla Prabhupāda: Yes—in the animal kingdom. But the civilized human being, the religious human being, is not meant to kill and eat animals. If you stop killing animals and chant the holy name of Christ, everything will be perfect. . . . I think the Christian priests should cooperate with the Kṛṣṇa consciousness movement. They should chant the name Christ or Christos and should stop condoning the slaughter of animals. This program follows the teachings of the Bible; it is not my philosophy. Please act accordingly and you will see how the world situation will change.

Science of Self-Realization (pp. 129–33)

Physical Effects of Meat-Eating

Ample food grains can be produced through agricultural enterprises, and profuse milk, yogurt, and ghee can be arranged through cow protection. Abundant honey can be obtained if the forests are protected. Unfortunately, in modern civilization, men are busy killing the cows that are the source of yogurt, milk, and ghee; they are cutting down all the trees that supply honey, and they are opening factories to manufacture nuts, bolts, automobiles, and wine instead of engaging in agriculture. How can the people be happy? They must suffer from all the misery of materialism. Their bodies become wrinkled and gradually deteriorate until they become almost like dwarves, and a bad odor emanates from their bodies because of unclean perspiration resulting from eating all kinds of nasty things. This is not human civilization.

Śrīmad-Bhāgavatam (5.16.25)

Vegetarians Are Also Committing Violence

Sometimes the question is put before us: "You ask us not to eat meat, but you are eating vegetables. Do you think that is not violence?" The answer is that eating vegetables is violence, and vegetarians are also committing violence against other living entities because vegetables also have life. Nondevotees are killing cows, goats, and so many other animals for eating purposes, and one who is vegetarian is also killing. . . . that is the law of nature. *Jīvo jīvasya jīvanam*: one living entity is the life for another living entity. But for a human being that violence should be committed only as much as necessary.

Śrīmad-Bhāgavatam (3.29.15)

The Cow Should Be Protected

Milk is compared to nectar, which one can drink to become immortal. Of course, simply drinking milk will not make one immortal, but it can increase the duration of one's life. In modern civilization, men do not think milk to be important, and therefore they do not live very long. Although in this age men can live up to one hundred years, their duration of life is reduced because they do not drink large quantities of milk. . . . Instead of drinking milk, people prefer to slaughter an animal and eat its flesh. [*Editors' note: Beef has six times the cholesterol of milk. High cholesterol causes heart disease, America's major cause of death.*] The Supreme Personality of Godhead, in His instructions of *Bhagavad-gītā*, advises *gorākṣya*, which means cow protection. The cow should be protected, milk should be drawn from the cows, and this milk should be prepared in various ways. One should take ample milk, and thus one can prolong one's life, develop his brain, execute devotional service, and ultimately attain the favor of the Supeme Personality of Godhead.

Śrīmad-Bhāgavatam (8.6.12)

Prasādam Frees One from Material Contamination

When there is an epidemic disease, an antiseptic vaccine protects a person from the attack of such an epidemic. Similarly, food offered to Lord Viṣṇu [Kṛṣṇa] and then taken by us makes us sufficiently resistant to material affection, and one who is accustomed to this practice is called a devotee of the Lord. Therefore, a person in Kṛṣṇa consciousness, who eats only food offered to Kṛṣṇa, can counteract all reactions of past material infections, which are impediments to the progress of self-realization. On the other hand, one who does not do so continues to increase the volume of sinful action, and this prepares the next body to resemble hogs and dogs, to suffer the resultant reactions of all sins. The material world is full of contaminations, and one who is immunized by accepting *prasādam* of the Lord (food offered to Viṣṇu) is saved from the attack, whereas one who does not do so become subjected to contamination.

Bhagavad-gītā (3.14)

Those Who Kill Will Be Killed

If one kills many thousands of animals in a professional way so that other people can purchase the meat to eat, one must be ready to be killed in a similar way in his next life and in life after life. There are many rascals who violate their own religious principles. According to Judeo-Christian scriptures, it is clearly said, "Thou shalt not kill." Nonetheless, giving all kinds of excuses, even the heads of religions indulge in killing animals while trying to pass as saintly persons. This mockery and hypocrisy in human society bring about unlimited calamities; therefore occasionally there are great wars. Masses of such people go out onto battlefields and kill themselves. Presently they have discovered the atomic bomb, which is simply awaiting wholesale destruction.

Caitanya-caritāmṛta (*Madhya* 24.251)

Showing Devotion to God by Offering Food with Love

It is prescribed in *Bhagavad-gītā*: "If a devotee offers Me a small flower, a leaf, some water, or a little fruit, I will accept it." The real purpose is to exhibit one's loving devotion to the Lord; the offerings themselves are secondary. If one has not developed loving devotion to the Lord and simply offers many kinds of foodstuffs, fruits, and flowers without real devotion, the offering will not be accepted by the Lord. We cannot bribe the Personality of Godhead. He is so great that our bribery has no value. Nor has He any scarcity; since He is full in Himself, what can we offer Him? Everything is produced by Him. We simply offer to show our love and gratitude to the Lord.

Śrīmad-Bhāgavatam (3.29.24)

Animal-Killing Is Not Civilized

Civilized men know the art of preparing nutritious foods from milk. For instance, on our New Vrindaban farm in West Virginia [*and on the other ISKCON farms throughout the world*], we make hundreds of first-class preparations from milk. Whenever visitors come, they are astonished that from milk such nice foods can be prepared. The blood of the cow is very nutritious, but civilized men utilize it in the form of milk. Milk is nothing but cow's blood transformed. You can make milk into so many things—yogurt, curd, ghee (clarified butter), and so on—and by combining these milk products with grains, fruits, and vegetables, you can make hundreds of preparations. This is civilized life—not directly killing an animal and eating its flesh.

Science of Self-Realization (p. 14)

Offering Food to Kṛṣṇa Is an Exchange of Love

Kṛṣṇa is so kind that if anyone offers Him a leaf, a flower, fruit, or some water, He will immediately accept it. The only condition is that these things should be offered with *bhakti* [devotion]. Otherwise, if one is puffed up with false prestige, thinking, "I have so much opulence, and I am giving something to Kṛṣṇa," one's offering will not be accepted by Kṛṣṇa. . . . for anything offered to Kṛṣṇa with love and affection, Kṛṣṇa can reciprocate many millions of times over, both materially and spiritually. The basic principle involved is an exchange of love. Therefore Kṛṣṇa teaches in *Bhagavad-gītā* (9.27): "O son of Kuntī, all that you do, all that you eat, all that you offer and give away, as well as all austerities that you may perform, should be done as an offering unto Me."

Śrīmad-Bhāgavatam (10.11.11)

Animals Also Have the Right to Life

Interviewer: Another point in the Declaration of Independence is that all men are endowed by God with certain natural rights that cannot be taken away from them. These are the rights of life, liberty, and . . .

Śrīla Prabhupāda: But animals also have the right to life. Why don't animals also have the right to live? The rabbits, for instance, are living in their own way in the forest. Why does the government allow hunters to go and shoot them?

Interviewer: They were simply talking about human beings.

Śrīla Prabhupāda: Then they have no real philosophy. The narrow idea that my family or my brother is good, and that I can kill all others, is criminal. Suppose that for my family's sake I kill your father. Is that philosophy? Real philosophy is *suhṛdaṁ sarva-bhūtānām*: friendliness to all living entities.

Science of Self-Realization (p. 209)

Satan's Philosophy

To be nonviolent to human beings and to be a killer or enemy of the poor animals is Satan's philosophy. In this age there is always enmity against poor animals, and therefore the poor creatures are always anxious. The reaction of the poor animals is being forced on human society, and therefore there is always the strain of cold or hot war between men, individually, collectively or nationally.

Śrīmad-Bhāgavatam (1.10.6)

Do Animals Have Souls?

Śrīla Prabhupāda: Some people say, "We believe that animals have no soul." That is not correct. They believe animals have no soul because they want to eat the animals, but actually animals do have a soul.

Reporter: How do you know that the animal has a soul?

Śrīla Prabhupāda: You can know, also. Here is the scientific proof. . . .the animal is eating, you are eating; the animal is sleeping, you are sleeping; the animal is defending, you are defending; the animal is having sex, you are having sex; the animals have children, you have children; they have a living place, you have a living place. If the animal's body is cut, there is blood; if your body is cut, there is blood. So, all these similarities are there. Now, why do you deny this one similarity, the presence of the soul? That is not logical. You have studied logic? In logic there is something called analogy. Analogy means drawing a conclusion by finding many points of similarity. If there are so many points of similarity between human beings and animals, why deny one similarity? That is not logic. That is not science.

Science of Self-Realization (pp. 35–36)

The Danger of Starvation

In *Bhagavad-gītā* it is confirmed that one who takes foodstuff after a performance of sacrifice eats real food for proper maintenance of the body and soul, but one who cooks for himself and does not perform any sacrifice eats only lumps of sin in the shape of foodstuffs. Such sinful eating can never make one happy or free from scarcity.

Famine is not due to an increase in population, as less intelligent economists think. When human society is grateful to the Lord for all His gifts for the maintenance of the living entities, then there is certainly no scarcity or want in society. But when men are unaware of the intrinsic value of such gifts from the Lord, surely they are in want. A person who has no God consciousness may live in opulence for the time being due to his past virtuous acts, but if one forgets his relationship with the Lord, certainly he must await the stage of starvation by the law of the powerful material nature.

Śrīmad-Bhāgavatam (3.5.49)

Killers of Animals Are Stone-hearted

Some rascals put forward the theory that an animal has no soul or is something like dead stone. In this way they rationalize that there is no sin in animal killing. Actually animals are not dead stone, but the killers of animals are stone-hearted. Consequently no reason or philosophy appeals to them. They continue keeping slaughterhouses and killing animals in the forest.

Śrīmad-Bhāgavatam (4.26.9)

The Animal Killer Will Become an Animal and Be Killed

By killing animals, not only will we be bereft of the human form but we will have to take an animal form and somehow or other be killed by the same type of animal we have killed. This is the law of nature. The Sanskrit word *māṁsa* means "meat." It is said: *māṁ saḥ khādatīti māṁsaḥ.* That is, " I am now eating the flesh of an animal who will some day in the future be eating my flesh."

Caitanya-caritāmṛta (*Madhya* 24.252)

Whether in the Name of Religion or for Food, Animal Slaughter Is Condemned

Animal sacrifice in the name of religion is current practically all over the world in every established religion. It is said that Lord Jesus Christ, when twelve years old, was shocked to see the Jews sacrificing birds and animals in the synagogues and that he therefore rejected the Jewish system of religion and started the religious system of Christianity, adhering to the Old Testament commandment "Thou shalt not kill." At the present day, however, not only are animals killed in the name of sacrifice, but the killing of animals has increased enormously because of the increasing number of slaughterhouses. Slaughtering animals, either for religion or for food, is most abominable and is condemned.

Śrīmad-Bhāgavatam (7.15.10)

There Is Already Enough Food

As human society is presently structured, there is sufficient production of grains all over the world. Therefore the opening of slaughterhouses cannot be supported. In some nations there is so much surplus grain that sometimes extra grain is thrown into the sea, and sometimes the government forbids further production of grain. The conclusion is that the earth produces sufficient grain to feed the entire population, but the distribution of this grain is restricted due to trade regulations and a desire for profit. Consequently in some places there is scarcity of grain and in others profuse production. If there were one government on the surface of the earth to handle the distribution of grain, there would be no question of scarcity, no necessity to open slaughterhouses, and no need to present false theories about overpopulation.

Śrīmad-Bhāgavatam (4.17.25)

A Diet to Cure the Disease of the Soul

Everyone should know that there are two kinds of diseases in human society. One disease, which is called *adhyātmika*, or material disease, pertains to the body, but the main disease is spiritual. The living entity is eternal, but somehow or other, when in contact with the material energy, he is subjected to the repetition of birth, death, old age, and disease. . . . The Kṛṣṇa consciousness movement has taken up the mission of curing this disease, but people are not very appreciative because they do not know what this disease is. A diseased person needs both proper medicine and a proper diet, and therefore the Kṛṣṇa consciousness movement supplies materially stricken people with the medicine of the chanting of the holy name, or the Hare Kṛṣṇa *mahā-mantra*, and the diet of *prasādam* [vegetarian foods offered to Lord Kṛṣṇa].

Caitanya-caritāmṛta (*Ādi* 10.51)

Elevation to the Transcendental Position

Our Kṛṣṇa consciousness movement acts on this principle. We simply give people the chance to hear about the Supreme Personality of Godhead and give them *prasādam* to eat, and the actual result is that all over the world people are responding to this process and becoming pure devotees of Lord Kṛṣṇa. We open hundreds of centers all over the world just to give people in general a chance to hear about Kṛṣṇa and accept Kṛṣṇa's *prasādam*. These two processes can be accepted by anyone, even a child. It doesn't matter whether one is poor or rich, learned or foolish, black or white, old or still a child—anyone who simply hears about the Supreme Personality of Godhead and takes *prasādam* is certainly elevated to the transcendental position of devotional service.

Caitanya-caritāmṛta (*Ādi* 7.141)

Spiritual Food

A flower accepted for one's sense gratification is material, but when the same flower is offered to the Supreme Personality of Godhead by a devotee, it is spiritual. Food taken and cooked for oneself is material, but food cooked for the Supreme is spiritual *prasādam*. This is a question of realization.

Śrīmad-Bhāgavatam (8.12.8)

An Ideal Diet

The purpose of food is to increase the duration of life, purify the mind, and aid bodily strength. This is its only purpose. In the past, great authorities selected those foods that best aid health and increase life's duration, such as milk products, sugar, rice, wheat, fruits, and vegetables.

Animal fat is available in the form of milk, which is the most wonderful of all foods. Milk, butter, cheese, and similar products give animal fat in a form which rules out any need for the killing of innocent creatures. . . . Protein is amply available through split peas, *dāl,* whole wheat, etc.

The best food is the remnant of what is offered to the Supreme Personality of Godhead. In *Bhagavad-gītā* the Supreme Lord says that He accepts preparations of vegetables, flour, and milk when offered with devotion. Of course, devotion and love are the chief things which the Supreme Personality of Godhead accepts.

Therefore to make food antiseptic, eatable, and palatable for all persons, one should offer food to the Supreme Personality of Godhead.

Bhagavad-gītā (17.8–10)

Food Offered to Kṛṣṇa Becomes Transcendental

In *Bhagavad-gītā* (9.26) Kṛṣṇa says, "If one offers Me with love and devotion a leaf, a flower, fruit, or water, I will accept it." The Lord is *pūrṇa,* complete, and therefore He eats everything offered by His devotees. However, by the touch of His transcendental hand, all the food remains exactly as before. It is the quality that is changed. Before the food was offered, it was something else, but after it is offered the food acquires a transcendental quality. Because the Lord is *pūrṇa,* He remains the same even after eating. The food offered to Kṛṣṇa is qualitatively as good as Kṛṣṇa; just as Kṛṣṇa is *avyaya,* indestructible, the food eaten by Kṛṣṇa, being identical with Him, remains as before. Apart from this, Kṛṣṇa can eat the food with any one of His transcendental senses. He can eat by seeing the food, or by touching it. Nor should one think that it is necessary for Kṛṣṇa to eat. He does not become hungry like an ordinary human being; nonetheless, He presents Himself as being hungry, and as such, He can eat everything and anything, regardless of quantity.

Caitanya-caritāmṛta (*Ādi* 4.78)

7

Recipes

Remember . . .
After preparing any of these recipes, please offer the food
to Lord Kṛṣṇa before serving. Here is a summary of the
procedure.

1. Do not taste the food while cooking.
2. After cooking, place the food on a plate for offering to
Kṛṣṇa. This plate should not be used for any other
purpose.
3. Set the plate before a picture of Lord Kṛṣṇa. You may
use the one in the color section of this book.
4. In a devotional mood, ask the Lord to please accept
your offering.
5. Repeat several times the Hare Kṛṣṇa *mahā-mantra*—
Hare Kṛṣṇa, Hare Kṛṣṇa, Kṛṣṇa Kṛṣṇa, Hare Hare/ Hare
Rāma, Hare Rāma, Rāma Rāma, Hare Hare.
6. Afterwards, remove the food from the offering plate.
This food and any food remaining in the cooking pots
may now be served.

See Chapter 5 for more details.

Notes on Ingredients

Almost all of the ingredients in this cookbook will be familiar to you and readily available at most food stores. A very few items, however, may have to be purchased at specialty shops.

- *hing*—also known as asafetida, this spice is used in several of the recipes and can serve as a substitute for garlic and onions, which are not offerable to Lord Kṛṣṇa. Hing may be purchased at most Indian, Chinese, or Middle Eastern specialty shops.
- *garam masala*—a mixture of spices, typically including ground coriander, ground cumin, and ginger, available from Indian specialty shops.
- *garbanzo bean flour*—available at Indian specialty shops, where it is called "besan flour." Garbanzo bean (or chickpea) flour may also be found at Middle Eastern specialty shops.
- *tofu*—this protein-rich, cheeselike substance prepared from soybeans is available from most health food stores and Oriental specialty shops.
- *Chinese sesame oil*—this roasted sesame seed oil, with its unique nutty flavor, is available from most Oriental specialty shops.
- *filo*—thin sheets of pastry available from Middle Eastern or Greek specialty shops.

Specially Prepared Ingredients

Curd and ghee are two easy-to-make basic ingredients of many recipes found in *A Higher Taste*. They have no substitute. Curd is a light, natural, protein-rich cheese. Ghee is the purified essence of butter. The butter you bring home from the store is eighty-percent butterfat, eighteen-percent water, and two-percent protein solids. If you slowly cook the butter, the water boils off and the protein solids separate from the butterfat. Finally, you are left with a golden liquid that you can use for deep-frying. The advantage of ghee is that it does not smoke, bubble, or burn, as butter does, at high temperatures. Also, ghee does not require refrigeration for storage. No cooking oil can match ghee for its pleasant taste and ease of digestion.

Ghee

Place five pounds of butter into a large, heavy saucepan. Heat over medium-high heat, stirring occasionally, until the butter melts and comes to a boil. When the surface of the butter is covered with a frothy white foam, reduce the heat to a very low temperature. Simmer, uncovered and undisturbed, until the gelatinous protein solids have collected on the bottom of the pan, and a thin layer of pale golden, crusty solids has formed on the surface. The cooking time will be about three hours. With a wire-meshed skimmer, skim off the thin crust on the surface. (If you don't have one, you can use a large, metal spoon.) The ideal finished ghee is crystal clear and pale gold in color. Ghee becomes dark when it is cooked on excessively high heat or is cooked too long.

Arrange a strainer, lined with three thicknesses of cheesecloth or one thickness of good quality paper towel over a large pan or bowl. Don't use paper towels with plastic reinforcing threads, as the plastic will melt. Ladle the clear ghee through the filter system to collect the protein solids from the ghee until you have ladled off as much clear ghee as you can without disturbing the milky solids on the bottom of the pan. These solids may be discarded.

Be sure to cool the ghee to room temperature before covering. Store in an airtight container in a cool, dark, dry place, or refrigerate. Ghee that has been well purified, filtered, and properly stored will last for months. After ghee has been used for cooking it can be strained and stored in the same manner.

Making Curd

½ gallon milk
5 tablespoons strained lemon juice

In 1-gallon pot heat milk on high heat, stirring occasionally, making sure that milk is not sticking to bottom of pan. Bring to a boil. Lower heat and add lemon juice.

Stir gently around sides of pan until all the milk has separated into curds and whey. The liquid (whey) should be clear. If not, add a little more lemon juice. Turn off heat.

In a colander place cheesecloth and strain curd. (Whey can be used in soups.) Rinse the curd with cold water.

Gather up sides of cheesecloth and twist to seal curd tightly inside. Put something heavy on top of the curd to press it (a heavy stone or a pot filled with water).

Keep the weight on anywhere from 15 minutes to 2 hours, depending on the recipe.

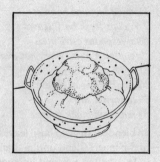

Italian Dinner (#1)

Pesto
Stuffed Eggplant
Herb Rolls
Batter-Fried Mozzarella
Vegetable Salad
Lemon Sherbet

Pesto

1 pound linguine noodles
2 ½ cups fresh basil leaves
6 tablespoons olive oil
⅓ cup pine nuts (when not available, blanched almonds may be used)
¾ cup Parmesan cheese
¾ teaspoon salt
¾ teaspoon black pepper

In blender crush up basil leaves, olive oil, pine nuts, cheese, salt, and pepper. Blend until a thick sauce.

In 1-gallon pot add linguine to boiling water to which you have added ½ teaspoon salt. Boil linguine 10 minutes until the pasta is cooked. Drain thoroughly. Rinse with cold water. Put pasta in a warm serving dish, and spoon pesto sauce over pasta. Serve immediately.

Serves 4.

Stuffed Eggplant

2 eggplants (cut in half, lengthwise)
1 small can of tomato puree (8 oz.)
1 cup bread crumbs
2 zucchini (chopped in ¼-inch cubes)
1 pound mozzarella cheese (grated)
1 ½ cups oil or ghee
1 ½ teaspoons black pepper
1 ½ teaspoons salt
¼ teaspoon hing
1 teaspoon lemon juice
1 tablespoon basil leaves
1 tablespoon oregano flakes

In large skillet heat 1 cup oil or ghee. Cut eggplants lengthwise in equal halves. Place all four halves of eggplants face down in hot oil. Adjust to low heat. Cook eggplant for about 10 minutes on each side or until very tender. It's ready when you can push a knife point through easily. Turn off flame and set aside.

In one-quart saucepan add ¼ cup of oil or ghee. When heated add 1 teaspoon black pepper, hing, and lemon juice. Quickly add tomato puree. Add ½ cup water, 1 teaspoon salt, and basil leaves. Cook on medium heat for ½ hour, stirring often.

In small skillet add last ¼ cup of oil or ghee. When hot add ½ teaspoon black pepper. Quickly add chopped zucchini, add ½ teaspoon salt, and fry at high heat for 5 minutes, stirring frequently. Add bread crumbs and lower heat. (Spiced bread crumbs may be used, but then refrain from using salt.) Cook for 2 more minutes.

Return to skillet with cooked eggplants. Divide zucchini stuffing in four parts, put evenly on top of eggplants, and cover with sauce and grated cheese. Cover and put on a low flame until cheese is melted. Garnish with parsley and oregano. Serve hot.
    Serves 4.

Herb Rolls

2 tablespoons yeast
1 ½ cups warm water (105°)
⅓ cup buttermilk
1 tablespoon sugar
1 teaspoons salt
½ cup melted butter
3 cups flour
1 teaspoon oregano
1 ½ teaspoons basil leaves
1 tablespoon chopped parsley
¼ teaspoon hing

In large bowl add yeast to water and let sit for 30 seconds. Add melted butter, spices, buttermilk, salt, and sugar.

Gradually stir in flour and knead for 8 minutes. If too wet add a little more flour.

Grease large bowl with a little butter and add dough. Cover and let rise in warm kitchen area until doubled in bulk (approximately 45 minutes). Fold dough over, punch down, and knead 1 minute.

Preheat oven to 375°. Grease muffin pans.

Make 36 small balls about 1-inch each. Fill greased muffin tins with 3 balls each. They will look like a cloverleaf.

Cover and let rise for 1 hour.

Bake for 15 minutes or until golden brown. Serve hot with butter.

Makes 1 dozen rolls.

Govinda's Natural Foods Restaurant in Los Angeles, one of the Hare Kṛṣṇa movement's many fine gourmet vegetarian restaurants.

Sweet-and-Sour Tofu Vegetable (p. 110).

Recipe Photos/Norwood

Spaghetti and Vegetarian Kofta Balls in Tomato Sauce (p. 88).

At left: Eggplant, Tomato, and Panir (p. 94); Cashew Rice with Peas (p. 95); and Puris (p. 98).

Below: Vegetable Quiche (p. 123).

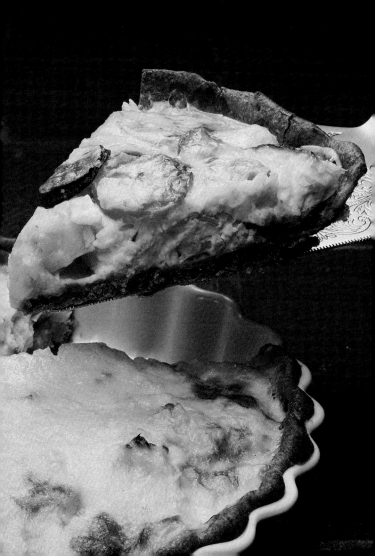

Leonardo da Vinci

Benjamin Franklin

Count Leo Tolstoy

George Bernard Shaw

Four Famous Vegetarians

Seeing the soul and the accompanying Supersoul within animals as well as humans, the self-realized sage behaves kindly to them all.

Lord Kṛṣṇa

"If one offers Me with love and devotion a leaf, a flower, fruit, or water, I will accept it."

Bhagavad-gītā (9.26)

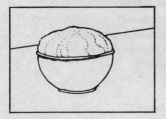

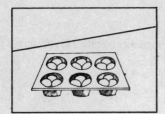

Batter-Fried Mozzarella

1 pound mozzarella cheese (cut in 1 ½ inch cubes)
flour for coating
1 cup buttermilk
bread crumbs for coating (spiced)
oil or ghee for deep frying
basil leaves for garnishing

Coat the cheese in flour, dip into the buttermilk, then into the bread crumbs. Repeat the process.

Deep fry cubes a few at a time in hot oil or ghee until golden brown. Drain on absorbent paper. Serve hot, garnished with basil leaves.

This can also be served with a sweet-and-sour sauce, or tomato chutney (see page 99).

Serves 4.

Vegetable Salad

1 8-ounce can pitted black olives (drained)
1 16-ounce can water-packed artichoke hearts (drained)
½ pound hard Italian cheese (cut in ½-inch slices)
3 medium size tomatoes (cut in eighths)
3 tablespoons olive oil
1 ½ teaspoons lemon juice
2 teaspoons chopped fresh basil leaves
½ teaspoon salt
½ teaspoon black pepper
pinch of hing

In bowl combine all of the above ingredients and set in refrigerator for 1 hour before serving.
   Serves 4.

Lemon Sherbet

1 cup whipping cream
1 cup yogurt (plain)
⅔ cup sugar
juice from 1 lemon
a drop of yellow food coloring (if desired)
1 ½ teaspoons grated lemon peel

In bowl combine whipping cream and sugar. Whip with mixer on high speed until cream is stiff. Fold in lemon juice, yogurt, and lemon peel. Add coloring at this time if desired. Put in freezer. Stir every 45 minutes until frozen (about 5 hours).
   Serves 4.

Italian Dinner (#2)

Minestrone Soup
Kofta Balls in Tomato Sauce
Breaded Zucchini Sticks
Green Beans and Tomato
Calzone
Neapolitan Cheesecake

Minestrone Soup

2 tablespoons olive oil
1 cup tomato (skinned and chopped)
⅓ cup garbanzo beans (soaked overnight)
¼ cup basil leaves
1 parsley sprig (chopped)
9 cups water
1 carrot (peeled and diced)
1 celery stalk (diced)
1 cup diced potatoes
1 large zucchini (diced)
1 cup shredded cabbage
salt
freshly ground pepper
½ cup barley
½ cup Parmesan cheese
½ teaspoon hing

Heat oil in large saucepan, add hing and cabbage. Sauté for 1 minute. Add tomatoes, chick-peas, basil, parsley, and water. Bring to a boil, cover, and simmer for 1 hour.

Add carrots and celery, and cook for 20 more minutes.

Add remaining ingredients, except for cheese. Cook 45 more minutes. Add salt to taste.

Let the soup stand for 15 minutes. Stir in Parmesan cheese and serve hot.

Serves 6.

Kofta Balls in Tomato Sauce

Sauce:

3 pounds tomatoes, blended (preferably Italian, plum type)
1/4 cup olive oil
2 tablespoons butter
1/2 teaspoon hing
1 medium carrot, cut in 8 pieces
2 teaspoons sweet basil
2 teaspoons salt
1 teaspoon turbinado sugar
1/4 teaspoon black pepper
2 bay leaves
1 pound spaghetti

Heat oil and butter over medium heat. Add hing and fry for 30 seconds. Add carrot pieces and fry for 1 minute. Stir in the blended tomatoes and the remaining seasonings. Raise the heat and bring to a boil, then reduce the heat and simmer for 1 hour. Remove carrot pieces and bay leaves.

Kofta:

2 cups grated cauliflower
2 cups grated cabbage
1 1/2 cups garbanzo bean flour
1 1/2 teaspoons salt
1/2 teaspoon hing
1 teaspoon garam masala
1 teaspoon ground cumin
1/2 teaspoon corriander powder
1/2 teaspoon turmeric
pinch of cayenne
ghee or oil for deep frying

Heat ghee in a wok or 2-quart saucepan. Combine all of the ingredients in a bowl. Roll in 24 balls, 1 inch in diameter. Place as many balls in the ghee as possible, leaving enough room for them to float comfortably. Fry over medium heat for 10 minutes, until the kofta is a rich golden brown. Drain in colander.

Place the kofta in the tomato sauce 5 minutes before serving. If after sitting the kofta soaks up most of the sauce, add a little water to produce more liquid.

Cook spaghetti as directed on box. Serve kofta and sauce over spaghetti.

Serves 4.

Breaded Zucchini Sticks

3 zucchini
1 cup flour
½ cup bread crumbs
1 ½ cups water
½ teaspoon salt
1 teaspoon basil leaves
pinch of black pepper
pinch of hing
oil for frying

Quarter zucchini lengthwise and cut each piece in half.

In bowl combine flour, bread crumbs, and spices. Add water and stir.

Fill skillet ⅓ full with oil and then heat. Dip zucchini pieces in batter and then into hot oil. Fry on all sides until tender and crisp. Serve hot.

Serves 4.

Green Beans and Tomato

1 ½ pounds green beans (cut in half)
1 large tomato (skinned and chopped)
4 tablespoons olive oil
½ teaspoon salt
¼ teaspoon freshly ground pepper
pinch of hing

Heat oil in nonstick skillet. Add hing. Stir in tomato, then add beans. Add enough water to barely cover beans. Add salt and pepper, and bring to a boil. Cover and lower heat. Simmer for 15 minutes or until beans are tender. Remove cover and increase heat to thicken the liquid (about 3 minutes). Serve warm or cool.
   Serves 4.

Calzone

Dough:

2 tablespoons yeast
1 cup warm water (105°)
1 teaspoon salt
⅓ cup oil (not olive oil)
2 cups flour

Filling:

⅓ cup chopped mozzarella cheese
½ cup Parmesan cheese
1 ½ cups ricotta cheese
⅓ cup chopped parsley
1 cup deep fried eggplant cubes
2 teaspoons salt
1 teaspoon pepper
¼ teaspoon hing
oil for deep frying

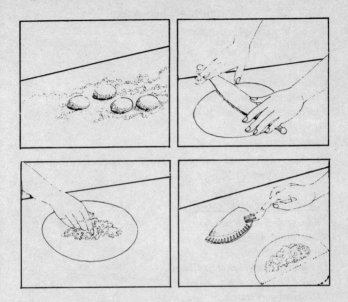

Add yeast to warm water and let sit for 1 minute. Add salt, oil, and flour. Knead for 3 minutes.

Sprinkle tabletop with flour. Separate dough into 2-inch balls. Cover with damp cloth and let them rise for 45 minutes.

While dough is rising mix all the filling ingredients together. Heat oil in wok until very hot.

Roll out balls into 6-inch circles. Divide stuffing into 8 portions. Place stuffing in center and fold over. Place fork in flour and use to seal edges. Fry in hot oil for about 1 minute on each side until they are reddish brown. Serve hot.

Makes 8.

Neapolitan Cheesecake

Use a 8 ½ inch springform pan.
　Preheat oven to 375°.

Crust:

⅓ cup ground walnuts
1 ⅓ tablespoons melted butter
2 tablespoons turbinado sugar
¾ cup flour
2 tablespoons water

Combine ingredients and press down on bottom of buttered
springform pan.

Bottom layer of cake (carob):

4 tablespoons carob powder
⅓ cup whipping cream
½ cup sour cream
12 ounces cream cheese (softened)
½ cup turbinado sugar
1 teaspoon cornstarch

Blend all ingredients in a blender until smooth. Pour on top of
crust.

Middle layer of cake (vanilla):

1 ½ teaspoons vanilla
⅓ cup whipping cream
½ cup sour cream
12 ounces cream cheese (softened)
½ cup turbinado sugar
1 teaspoon cornstarch

Blend all ingredients in a blender until smooth. Pour gently over
carob layer.

Top layer of cake (strawberry)

3 tablespoons strawberry jam
½ teaspoon strawberry flavoring (optional)
⅓ cup whipping cream
½ cup sour cream
12 ounces cream cheese (softened)
½ cup turbinado sugar
1 teaspoon cornstarch

Blend all ingredients in blender until smooth. Pour gently over vanilla layer.

Bake in oven for 50 minutes. Let stand on cooling rack for ½ hour and then refrigerate for at least 3 hours. Serve cool.

Makes 12 slices.

Indian Dinner (#1)

Eggplant, Tomato, and Panir
Cashew Rice and Peas
Samosas
Cucumber Raita
Puris
Coconut Burfy

Eggplant, Tomato, and Panir

5 large, ripe tomatoes (quartered)
½ cup water
1 large eggplant (cut in 1-inch cubes)
ghee for deep frying
½ tablespoon minced fresh ginger
½ teaspoon minced fresh chili
1 ½ teaspoons black mustard seeds
¼ teaspoon hing
pinch of turmeric
1 teaspoon ground coriander
1 teaspoon garam masala
1 teaspoon turbinado sugar
2 teaspoons salt
6 cups milk

From milk, make curd (see recipe, page 80). Press for 20 minutes. Cut curd into ½-inch cubes and deep fry until golden.

Place the tomatoes and water in a covered saucepan. Simmer for 15 minutes. Pour the contents through a sieve and strain into a bowl. Discard seeds and skin.

In a wok heat ghee to medium hot temperature. Deep fry eggplant cubes until golden brown and tender. Set colander over bowl. Drain eggplant. Save ghee.

The ghee that has been drained off the eggplant can be used to fry the spices. In a large frying pan heat the ghee over high heat for 30 seconds. Stir in ginger, chili, mustard seeds, and hing. Fry until the seeds start popping. Add tomato puree, remaining spices, and fried eggplant. Simmer uncovered for 8 minutes. Add panir (curd squares) and cover. Cook for 2 more minutes. Serve hot. Serves 4.

Cashew Rice with Peas

Basmati rice is a traditional Indian rice. It is imported from the East and may be purchased at all Indian grocery stores and most health food stores. White rice or brown rice may be used, but basmati rice is extra special in that it is nutritious and has a very good flavor.

1 cup basmati rice
½ cup roasted cashew pieces
½ cup peas
2 tablespoons ghee
pinch of turmeric
pinch of hing
½ teaspoon salt
1 ¾ cups water

Wash rice.

In 1-quart pan put 2 tablespoons ghee, hing, and rice. Stir over medium heat for 30 seconds. Add water, turmeric, and salt. Add peas. Bring to a full boil, then cover and cook on very low heat for 18 minutes. Stir in cashew pieces.

Garnish with coriander leaves.

Serves 4.

Samosas

2 cups cauliflower (cut in small pieces)
1 cup peas
ghee for deep frying
1 cup white flour
1 cup whole wheat flour
⅓ cup plus 3 tablespoons ghee
1 green chili (minced)
1 ½ teaspoons salt
1 teaspoon cumin seeds
1 teaspoon black mustard seeds
½ teaspoon turmeric
¼ teaspoon hing
1 tablespoon garam masala
1 teaspoon coriander powder

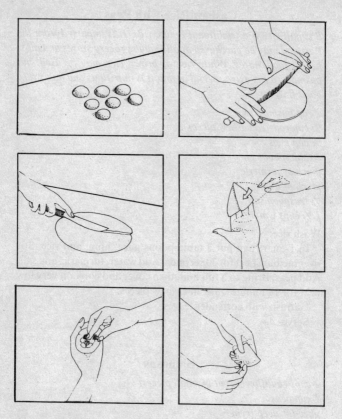

Steam cauliflower and peas until very tender.

In frying pan put 3 tablespoons ghee. Add green chili, black mustard seeds, and cumin seeds. When they begin to crackle add turmeric and hing. Add steamed vegetables, and all remaining spices. Mash vegetables and cook over medium heat until you have a thick paste for stuffing. This takes about 20 minutes. Cool.

Dough:

Combine flour with ⅓ cup ghee. Add enough water to make a rollable dough (about ½ cup).

Roll dough into twelve balls. With rolling pin roll each ball into a 5-inch circle. Cut the circles in half. Seal two ends together and put 1 tablespoon stuffing into each triangle. Seal edges and turn over, making decorative loops. Seal samosas tightly enough to hold together when frying.

Heat ghee in wok until it is medium hot. Add samosas and fry in ghee for 15–20 minutes, stirring and turning over occasionally. Serve hot.

Makes 2 dozen.

Cucumber Raita

1 cup yogurt
½ cup water
1 large cucumber (peeled and sliced in ¼-inch rounds)
1 teaspoon salt
¼ teaspoon cumin powder
¼ cup fresh coriander leaves

The best cumin powder to use for a raita is dry roasted. If you can take the time (just 5 minutes), bake the cumin seeds until they are a little dark, and then grind them in a spice grinder, or under a rolling pin. This process gives extra-special flavor.

In bowl mix yogurt, water, salt, and cayenne. Add cucumbers to yogurt mixture. Sprinkle cumin powder on top. Garnish with coriander leaves.

Serves 4.

Puris

1 cup white flour
1 cup whole wheat flour
⅓ cup ghee
½ cup water
ghee for deep frying

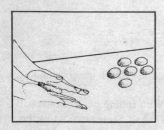

In bowl combine flour, ghee, and water. Knead for 3 minutes. If too wet add more flour.

Divide dough into 12 balls. Flatten balls in your palm. On tabletop, with a light rolling motion roll out each piece of dough into an even 4-inch circle.

Heat ghee or oil in wok. Ghee should be very hot. Put in 1 puri. It will drop to the bottom, then float to the top and puff up. Cook puri on both sides until golden. This takes about 45 seconds. Do not be discouraged if they do not always inflate.

Makes 1 dozen.

Coconut Burfi

4 cups milk
½ cup heavy cream
⅓ cup turbinado sugar
⅓ cup shredded or flaked coconut (unsweetened)
1 teaspoon vanilla

In large heavy saucepan (preferably nonstick) put milk and cream. Bring to a boil over medium-high heat, stirring occasionally to prevent sticking. Stirring often and scraping the bottom of the saucepan, keep the milk boiling (but reduce the heat if the milk starts to boil over). The milk will begin to thicken after approximately ½ hour. When the boiling action slows to a rolling boil, reduce heat and add the sugar and vanilla. Continue cooking, stirring constantly until a small amount of the mixture dropped into very cold water forms a small, soft ball. Stir in coconut and cook just 3 minutes longer.

Empty burfy onto a flat, buttered tray and mold into a square ½-inch thick. Cool at room temperature. Cut into desired portions.

This burfy can be made up to 2 days in advance of serving, but must be refrigerated. Remove from refrigerator 1 hour before serving.

Indian Dinner (#2)

Potato and Cabbage Vegetable
Mung Dal
Basmati Rice
Cauliflower Pakoras
Tomato Chutney
Chapatis
Bengali Kheer

Potato and Cabbage Vegetable

1 cabbage (sliced very thin)
3 large potatoes (cut in ½-inch cubes)
4 tablespoons ghee
1 small jalapeño chili (diced finely)
1 tablespoon black mustard seeds
¼ teaspoon turmeric
1 tablespoon coriander powder
1 teaspoon salt
1 small slice of lemon

In pan heat ghee, mustard seeds, chili, and turmeric. When mustard seeds start to crackle add potatoes. Stir for 8 minutes on medium heat. Add cabbage and cook for 15 more minutes until cabbage and potatoes are both tender. Add salt and coriander powder. Sprinkle with lemon juice. Serve hot.

Serves 4.

Mung Dal

Mung beans are split yellow mung beans, which can be purchased at all Indian grocery stores. If they are not available to you, you may use green split peas or yellow split peas with this same recipe.

1 cup beans
7 cups water
1 cup chopped tomatoes
1 medium zucchini (peeled and chopped in 1-inch cubes)
5 tablespoons ghee
½ tablespoon minced ginger
1 ½ tablespoons cumin seeds
1 tablespoon black mustard seeds
1 green chili (minced)
¼ teaspoon hing
1 ½ teaspoon turmeric
1 tablespoon salt
fresh coriander leaves for garnish

In 1-gallon saucepan put 3 tablespoons ghee, turmeric, hing, and beans. Fry for 30 seconds on medium heat. Add vegetables and fry for 1 more minute. Add water, salt, fresh chili, and diced ginger. Bring to a boil over high heat, then cover, lower heat, and let dal simmer for 1 hour or until the beans have dissolved into a thick soup. Set aside.

In small skillet add remaining ghee. When hot add cumin seeds and black mustard seeds. When the seeds start to crackle pour the mixture into the pot of dal. Garnish with fresh coriander leaves or parsley. Serve hot.

Serves 6.

Basmati Rice

1 ½ cups rice
2 tablespoons ghee (or butter)
½ teaspoon salt
½ teaspoon black pepper
2 ¾ cups water

In saucepan heat ghee and then add rice. Stir rice on medium heat for 1 minute. Add water and spices and bring to a boil. Cover and put on low heat to simmer for 18 minutes. Serve hot.
   Serves 4.

Cauliflower Pakoras

1 medium size cauliflower (cut into flowerets)
1 ½ cups garbanzo-bean flour
½ to ¾ cup water
1 teaspoon salt
1 teaspoon cumin powder
1 tablespoon coriander powder
pinch of cayenne
pinch of hing
½ teaspoon turmeric
1 teaspoon garam masala
ghee for deep frying

In bowl combine flour and spices. Add water until it becomes a medium-thick pancake batter.

   Heat ghee in wok until it is very hot.

   Dip cauliflower pieces in batter. Put pieces in hot ghee. They will first sink to the bottom of the wok and then rise. Fry for 5 minutes and then stir occassionally until they are a dark golden brown (about 15 minutes).

   Serve with tomato chutney. This recipe can also be used with potato, eggplant, or zucchini pieces.
   Serves 4.

Tomato Chutney

6 ripe tomatoes (cut in small pieces)
1 tablespoon ghee
1 small jalapeño chili (minced)
½ tablespoon mustard seeds
1 teaspoon grated fresh ginger
½ teaspoon salt
4 tablespoons turbinado sugar
1 tablespoon coriander powder

In skillet heat ghee, then add mustard seeds, chili, and ginger. Add tomato pieces. Cover and fry on medium heat for 15 minutes or until tomatoes have become a chunky sauce.

Remove from pan and put in blender on low speed for 5 seconds.

Put back in skillet and add salt, sugar, and coriander powder. Cook for 3 minutes uncovered. Serve hot or cold.

Serves 4.

Chapatis

2 cups whole wheat flour
⅓ cup yogurt
½ to ¾ cup water as needed
ghee or melted butter

In bowl combine flour and yogurt. Gradually add water until you have a soft dough. Knead on floured tabletop.

Divide dough into 12 pieces. Roll each piece into a ball and then press flat in the palms of your hands.

Place a cast iron skillet on medium heat, so it will be a little hot by the time you are ready to cook the first chapati.

Roll flattened balls into 5-inch circles on a table or board covered with flour. Try to make the chapati as round as possible. After it is rolled, place on skillet. When the chapati starts bubbling on one side, turn it over and cook on the other side. This takes about 20 seconds on each side.

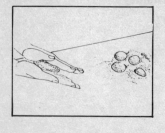
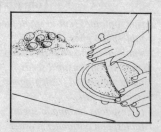

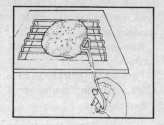

While first chapati is cooking in skillet, turn second burner on to medium heat. (If you have an electric range, use a small grill over the burner.)

After the chapati has been cooked in skillet, quickly take a pair of tongs and hold the chapati gently over medium heat until it puffs up. This should take about 5 seconds. Then hold chapati with tongs on other side and cook for another 5 seconds. Chapati will look like it is freckled with brown spots. Don't be discouraged if the chapati doesn't puff up all the time. This takes practice.

Brush with melted butter or ghee.

Makes 1 dozen.

Bengali Kheer (Rice Pudding)

6 cups milk
¾ cup rice
½ cup raisins
¼ teaspoon fresh cardamom powder
½ bay leaf
½ cup turbinado sugar

In large saucepan combine milk, rice, and bay leaf. Cook on high heat for 15 minutes, stirring very frequently. Bring to a rolling boil and then lower heat. Simmer for 40 more minutes until it thickens. Remove bay leaf and add sugar, raisins, and cardamom. Refrigerate until cold. Kheer thickens as it cools. Serve cool.

Serves 4.

Chinese Dinner (#1)

Hot-and-Sour Vegetable Soup
Manapua
Fried Rice
Sweet-and-Sour Tofu Vegetable
Almond Cookies

Hot-and-Sour Vegetable Soup

4 cups vegetable broth
2 tablespoons soy sauce
½ teaspoon salt (omit if broth is salted)
¼ teaspoon hing
½ teaspoon white pepper
½ cup corn kernels
1 cup shredded Chinese cabbage
½ cup chopped celery
½ pound diced tofu
2 tablespoons lemon juice
2 tablespoons cornstarch
¼ cup water
1 teaspoon sesame oil

In a 3-quart saucepan combine vegetable broth, soy sauce, and seasonings. Bring to a boil and add vegetables. Cover and simmer for 15 minutes. Add tofu and lemon juice, and cook uncovered for 5 minutes longer. Mix together cornstarch and ¼ cup water. Stir the paste into the soup, and continue to cook until the soup becomes slightly thicker, about 3 minutes. Mix in sesame oil and serve hot.

Serves 4.

Manapua

1 package dried yeast
1 cup warm water (105°)
1 tablespoon turbinado sugar
2 tablespoons salad oil
1 teaspoon salt
3 cups flour (1 unbleached white, 2 whole wheat)
Vegetable-cashew filling (recipe follows)
2 tablespoons butter

In large bowl dissolve yeast in warm water, add sugar, salt, and salad oil. Set aside for approximately 10 minutes, or until the mixture is bubbly. Stir in flour, a little at a time until the dough holds together. Turn dough onto a lightly floured board and knead until smooth and elastic (about 5 minutes). You may need to add a little flour to prevent sticking. Place dough into a lightly greased bowl, cover, and let rise in a warm place until doubled in bulk (about 50 minutes).

While the dough is rising the filling should be made.

Filling:

2 cups finely chopped broccoli
2 cups chopped Chinese cabbage
1 teaspoon minced fresh ginger
½ cup sliced water chestnuts
1 cup chopped cashews
¼ teaspoon hing
1 tablespoon oil
3 tablespoons soy sauce
1 teaspoon turbinado sugar
¼ cup water
1 tablespoon cornstarch
¼ teaspoon lemon juice
1 tablespoon Chinese sesame oil

In small bowl mix together soy sauce, sugar, water, cornstarch and lemon juice. Set aside.

. Heat 1 tablespoon oil in skillet. Add hing and fresh ginger. Fry for 1 minute. Stir in broccoli and cabbage and fry on high

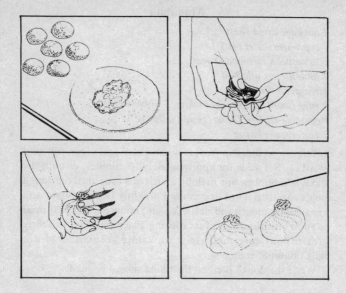

heat for 3 minutes. Mix in water chestnuts and cashews, and continue to fry for 3 minutes longer.

Pour the soy sauce mixture into the vegetables, and cook until the liquid thickens. This should take about 2 minutes. Remove from heat; mix in 1 tablespoon sesame oil, and cool.

When dough has risen, punch down and knead on lightly floured board for 1 minute.

Preheat oven to 350°.

Divide dough into 12 equal balls. Roll each ball into a 5-inch circle. Place two rounded tablespoons of filling in the center of each circle. Bring dough up around filling, pleating it as you pull it along. Twist to seal.

Place the buns 2 inches apart on a greased baking sheet. Cover and let rise for 30 minutes.

Bake at 350° for approximately 20 minutes, or until golden brown. Brush with butter and serve warm.

Makes 1 dozen.

Fried Rice

1 cup rice
2 cups water
7 tablespoons Chinese sesame oil
⅓ cup chopped tofu
½ cup bamboo shoots
1 medium carrot (coarsely grated)
1 small zucchini (chopped in fine pieces)
2 stalks celery (sliced in ½-inch slices)
1 cup thinly sliced cabbage
¼ pound fresh bean sprouts
¼ cup chopped almonds
2 teaspoons salt
1 tablespoon soy sauce
1 teaspoon grated fresh ginger
¼ teaspoon hing
1 tablespoon ground coriander

In 1-quart saucepan heat 1 tablespoon sesame oil, add rice, and fry for 30 seconds. Add water and ½ teaspoon salt and bring to a boil. Cover and cook on low heat for 18 minutes. Set aside.

In skillet heat 4 tablespoons sesame oil, grated ginger, and hing. Add carrots, zucchini, and celery. Cover and fry for 10 minutes on medium heat, stirring occasionally. Add cabbage, and fry for 5 more minutes uncovered. Add bean sprouts and bamboo shoots, and fry on high heat for 3 more minutes. Stir in soy sauce. Empty fried vegetables into a bowl.

In skillet heat remaining 2 tablespoons sesame oil. Add chopped almonds and chopped tofu and fry for 1 minute. Add rice and fry for 2 minutes on high heat. Sprinkle with ground coriander and remaining salt. Add to vegetables and stir gently.

Serves 4.

Sweet-and-Sour Tofu Vegetable

½ cup orange juice
½ cup apple juice
¼ cup lemon juice
2 tablespoons turbinado sugar
2 tablespoons cornstarch
½ pound firm tofu (cut in 1-inch cubes)
2 cups oil
3 tablespoons ghee or oil
1 tablespoon grated fresh ginger
¼ teaspoon hing
1 large green pepper (cut in ½-inch wide strips)
2 medium carrots (cut in 2-inch sticks)
2 medium zucchini
¼ pound Chinese pea pods (ends removed)
1 cup pineapple chunks (fresh, or canned in unsweetened juice)
⅓ cup water
3 tablespoons soy sauce
½ teaspoon salt
¼ teaspoon black pepper
1 tablespoon Chinese sesame oil

Combine orange, apple, and lemon juices, turbinado sugar, and cornstarch in a small bowl. Set aside.

In a small saucepan heat 2 cups oil. Fry tofu cubes until golden brown, about 5 minutes. Set aside.

Cut zucchini lengthwise in half, then slice in pieces ½-inch wide.

Heat 3 tablespoons oil in wok over medium heat, add ginger and hing. Fry for 30 seconds, then add pepper strips. After 2 minutes add carrots, zucchini, and pea pods, and stir fry for 3 minutes longer. Add water, soy sauce, salt, pepper, and pineapple chunks, if fresh. Cover and simmer for 8 minutes or just until vegetables are slightly tender.

Stir in fried tofu cubes and juice mixture. If canned fruit is being used it should also be added at this time. Stirring gently, cook until the sauce thickens, about 3 minutes. Remove from heat, stir in sesame oil, and serve immediately.

Serves 4.

Almond Cookies

½ cup soft butter
1 cup flour
⅓ cup turbinado sugar
3 tablespoons ground almonds
12 whole almonds
1 drop almond flavoring

Preheat oven to 350°.

Combine all above ingredients except whole almonds.

When thoroughly mixed, roll into 12 balls. Then press each ball firmly in palms of hands. Put one almond in the center of each cookie.

Place on ungreased cookie sheet. Bake for 10–12 minutes or until golden around edges.

Makes 1 dozen.

Chinese Dinner (#2)

Watercress Salad
Spring Rolls
Vegetable Lo Mein
Spicy Eggplant
Vanilla Ice Cream

Watercress Salad

1 small cauliflower
½ cup Chinese sesame oil
juice of 1 lemon
¼ teaspoon chervil
¼ teaspoon tarragon
¼ teaspoon basil leaves
¼ teaspoon dry mustard
salt and pepper to taste
2 bunches watercress (remove stems)
½ cup slivered almonds (roasted)
1   16-ounce can water-packed artichoke hearts (drained and sliced)

Cut cauliflower into small flowerets and steam for 5 minutes. Cool.

Place cauliflower, oil, lemon juice, and seasonings in a container. Cover and chill for at least 1 hour.

Place watercress leaves in colander and rinse with cold water. Drain excess water.

Arrange the leaves on 4 small plates. Place artichoke slices on watercress leaves. Pour cauliflower mixture on top of artichoke slices. Top with slivered almonds and serve.

Serves 4.

Spring Rolls

½ pound broccoli (cut in small flowerets)
2 cups Chinese cabbage (finely sliced)
1 cup bamboo shoots
1 cup sliced water chestnuts
¾ pound bean sprouts
1 cup chopped tofu
1 package eggless pastry wrappers (thawed)
5 tablespoons Chinese sesame oil
1 tablespoon minced fresh ginger
¼ teaspoon hing
¼ teaspoon black pepper
1 ½ tablespoons soy sauce
1 ½ teaspoons salt
1 ½ tablespoons ground coriander
4 cups oil for frying

In wok heat sesame oil, then add hing, fresh ginger, black pepper, and broccoli. Cover and cook on medium heat for 10 minutes. Add cabbage and fry for 3 more minutes. Add bamboo shoots, water chestnuts, and chopped tofu. Fry for 3 more minutes. Add bean sprouts, salt, ground coriander, and soy sauce. Fry for 2 more minutes. Put in colander to drain excess juices.

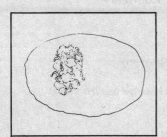
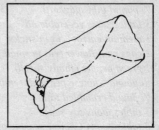

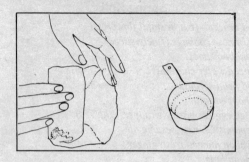

Heat 4 cups oil in wok.

Unwrap pastry. Have a small bowl of water handy to seal pastries. In center of pastry put 4 tablespoons stuffing. Fold sides over toward center, roll, and seal. Repeat with all 12 rolls.

Oil should be very hot. Fry each roll on each side for 30 seconds. They will be reddish brown. Drain on paper towels. Serve warm with a sweet-and-sour sauce if desired.

Makes 1 dozen.

Note: Eggless pastry wrappers may be purchased at Chinese, Thai, Philippine, or other specialty shops.

Vegetable Lo Mein

½ pound thin spaghetti
3 tablespoons vegetable oil
1 medium carrot (cut in sticks)
2 cups cauliflower (cut in small flowerets)
1 green pepper (thinly sliced)
¼ pound Chinese pea pods (ends removed and left whole)
½ pound crumbled tofu
3 tablespoons soy sauce
2 tablespoons Chinese sesame oil

Cook spaghetti, just until tender. Drain and rinse in cold water. Place in a large bowl, toss with 1 tablespoon oil, and refrigerate for 1 hour.

Combine all the vegetables with the tofu and set aside.

In wok heat 2 tablespoons oil and add spaghetti. Stir gently until it is evenly coated. Continue to fry the spaghetti over medium heat until lightly browned (about 5 minutes). Mix in the vegetables and tofu. Stir fry for 5 minutes longer. Add soy sauce, cover, and steam over low heat for 5 minutes. Remove lid, stir in sesame oil, and serve hot.

Serves 4.

Spicy Eggplant

2 medium eggplants (peeled and cut in ¼-inch strips)
1 tablespoon minced ginger
3 tablespoons vegetable oil
¼ teaspoon hing
1 green chili (minced)
1 teaspoon mustard powder
⅓ cup water
1 tablespoon Chinese sesame oil
1 tablespoon turbinado sugar
1 ½ teaspoons salt
1 ½ teaspoons lemon juice
1 ½ tablespoons soy sauce
1 teaspoon cornstarch

In wok heat oil, add ginger, hing, green chili, and mustard powder. Add eggplant, cover, and fry on high heat for 15 minutes, stirring occasionally.

In small bowl combine water, sesame oil, sugar, salt, lemon juice, soy sauce, and cornstarch. Add this sauce to eggplant and fry for 1 minute. Garnish with parsley or Chinese parsley leaves. Serve hot.

Serves 4.

Vanilla Ice Cream

1 ½ cups whipping cream
½ cup evaporated milk
½ cup yogurt
½ cup turbinado sugar
1 ½ teaspoons vanilla

In bowl combine whipping cream, sugar, and vanilla. Whip with mixer until stiff. Add evaporated milk and yogurt. Mix 30 seconds on low speed.

Cover and put in freezer. Stir every 45 minutes until frozen (about 5 hours).

Serves 4.

Mexican Dinner

Gazpacho
Avocado Salad
Enchiladas
Creamed Peas and Carrots
Mango Dessert

Gazpacho

2 cups tomato juice
2 cups vegetable stock, or 2 cups water and 2 vegetable boullion
 cubes
2 tablespoons lemon juice
1 teaspoon turbinado sugar
pinch of hing
pinch of cayenne
1 teaspoon salt
1 cucumber (peeled, seeded, and diced)
1 green pepper (diced)
4 medium tomatoes (peeled and coarsely chopped)

In 3 quart saucepan over medium heat combine tomato juice,
vegetable stock, lemon juice, sugar, hing, and cayenne. Leaving
the pot uncovered, bring the mixture to a boil. Stir in remaining
ingredients and again bring to a boil, uncovered. Remove from
heat and cool. Cover and chill.
 Serves 4.

Avocado Salad

Spicy Dressing (recipe follows)
2 ripe avocados
2 small tomatoes
1 cup pitted black olives
1 head butterhead lettuce

Cut avocados in small pieces and tomatoes in wedges. Place in a medium bowl along with the olives. Pour the salad dressing on and mix lightly. Marinate for at least ½ hour in the refrigerator. Serve on a bed of lettuce.

Spicy Dressing:

⅓ cup olive oil
juice of 1 ½ lemons
2 tablespoons tomato paste
1 teaspoon salt
1 teaspoon chili powder
½ teaspoon ground cumin
pinch of black pepper

Place all the ingredients in a blender, and blend on a low speed for 1 minute.
   Serves 4.

Enchiladas

Sauce:

1 large can tomato puree
1 small can tomato paste
¼ cup oil
1 small green chili (minced)
3 tablespoons ground cumin
2 tablespoons ground coriander
¼ teaspoon hing (optional)
2 teaspoons salt
2 teaspoons turbinado sugar

Heat oil in a saucepan, add chili, and fry for 30 seconds. Stir in ground spices and hing, frying for 30 seconds longer. Add tomato paste, and stir to soak up the oil and spices. Mix in the tomato puree, salt, and sugar. Simmer for 30 minutes.

Filling:

3 cups ricotta cheese
3 cups grated monterrey jack cheese
2 cups fresh corn kernels (2 ears)
1 bunch spinach (chopped)
½ teaspoon hing
1 tablespoon black pepper
2 teaspoons turbinado sugar
¼ teaspoon nutmeg
½ teaspoon salt (optional)
1 dozen corn tortillas
1 cup sour cream
oil for deep frying

Preheat oven to 350°

Steam corn for 8 minutes, add chopped spinach, and steam for 3 minutes longer. Drain excess water.

Heat oil over high heat. Fry tortillas one at a time for 15 seconds on each side. Use smooth-tipped tongs to flip the tortillas in the oil. Place on paper towels on a flat surface to cool. The tortilla should be pliable, not crispy.

In a large bowl mix together ricotta cheese, 2 cups grated cheese, vegetables, and seasonings. Place 3 tablespoons filling in a strip down the center of each tortilla. Roll each tortilla and place seam-down in a large, oiled baking pan. Cover with sauce and sprinkle with remaining grated cheese. Bake 15 minutes. Top each enchilada with 1 rounded tablespoon of sour cream.

Serves 4.

Creamed Peas and Carrots

3 cups peas (fresh or frozen)
5 tablespoons butter
2 medium carrots (peeled and diced)
pinch of hing
¼ teaspoon marjoram
¼ teaspoon thyme
salt and pepper to taste
1 tablespoon flour
1 cup light cream

Cover peas in lightly salted water and cook until tender. Drain and set aside. In a heavy pan melt 4 tablespoons butter, and add hing, carrots, and seasonings. Cover and cook over low heat, stirring occasionally, until carrots are tender, about 15 minutes.

In another small pan melt 1 tablespoon butter and stir in flour. Gently stir for 1 minute. Do not allow the mixture to brown. Gradually add cream, stirring constantly, until mixture is smooth and begins to boil. When the sauce has thickened remove from heat. This takes about 3 minutes.

Combine peas with seasoned carrots. Fold in the cream sauce and serve.

Serves 4.

Mango Dessert

3 ripe mangos (peeled and pitted)
15-ounce can sweetened condensed milk
juice from 1 lemon
1 cup raspberries (fresh or frozen)
¼ cup orange juice
4 tablespoons chopped pistachio nuts

Marinate raspberries in orange juice.

Place mangos, sweetened condensed milk, and lemon juice in a blender. Blend until smooth. Pour half of this mixture evenly into 4 dessert dishes. Divide ¾ cup raspberries evenly into the dishes, then add the remainder of the mango mixture. Chill for several hours.

Immediately before serving, top with remaining berries and garnish with pistachio nuts.

Serves 4.

French Dinner

Stuffed Tomatoes
Vegetable Quiche
Green Beans Almondine
Vegetable Rice Casserole
Fruit Juice Gel

Stuffed Tomatoes

4 large stuffing tomatoes
2 cups peeled and chopped potatoes (¼-inch cubes)
2 tablespoons ghee
2 tablespoons sour cream
1 tablespoon yogurt
1 tablespoon sesame seeds
1 teaspoon black mustard seeds
½ teaspoon salt
pinch of hing
¼ teaspoon black pepper
1 tablespoon prepared mustard

In skillet heat ghee, black mustard seeds, hing, and black pepper. Add potatoes, cover, and fry on medium heat for 10 minutes. Add sesame seeds and fry for 1 minute until the seeds are a little golden. Add sour cream, yogurt, mustard, and salt. Set aside.

Slice the tops off the tomatoes and scoop out the insides. Fill tomatoes with stuffing and cool. Garnish with parsley and paprika. Serve cold.

Serves 4.

Vegetable Quiche

1 cup cauliflower (cut in flowerets)
½ cup sliced carrots
¾ cup sliced zucchini
¾ cup water-packed artichoke hearts
12 ounces sour cream
½ cup Parmesan cheese
1 cup grated monterrey jack cheese
2 tablespoons cornstarch
3 teaspoons ghee
½ teaspoon hing (optional)
1 ½ teaspoons salt
¼ teaspoon black pepper
pinch of turmeric

<u>*Crust:*</u>

1 ½ cups whole wheat flour
½ cup melted butter
⅓ cup Parmesan cheese
3 tablespoons water

Blend together flour, cheese, and butter. Texture will resemble wet sand. Add water a little at a time. Pat mixture on bottom and along sides of 9-inch quiche pan. Bake at 400° for 8 minutes.

In frying skillet heat ghee and add hing. Add cauliflower and carrots, and stir until they are evenly coated. Cover and cook for 10 minutes over medium heat, stirring occasionally. Add zucchini and cook 5 more minutes.

In large bowl combine sour cream, cornstarch, salt, pepper, and turmeric. Add Parmesan cheese and ½ cup monterrey jack cheese. Fold in vegetables and artichoke hearts. Pour into quiche pan and top with remaining monterrey jack cheese. Bake at 400° for 40 minutes or until the edges of the quiche are dark and the center is slightly golden.

Allow the quiche to set about 30 minutes before cutting and serving.

Green Beans Almondine

1 ½ pounds fresh string beans
3 tablespoons ghee
¼ teaspoon hing
1 teaspoon salt
¼ teaspoon black pepper
1 teaspoon ground coriander
½ cup slivered almonds

Remove ends of green beans, and slice lengthwise in strips.

Heat ghee in heavy skillet, and add hing. Add green beans, salt, pepper, and 2 tablespoons water. Cover and cook on medium-low heat for 15 minutes. Remove cover and cook for 5 minutes or until all the water has evaporated. Add almonds and cook 5 minutes longer. Sprinkle with coriander powder.

Serves 4.

Vegetable Rice Casserole

4 cups cooked rice
1 ½ cups broccoli flowerets
1 medium carrot (sliced)
1 bunch spinach (chopped)
2 medium tomatoes (cut in eighths)
¼ cup olive oil
¼ teaspoon hing
⅓ cup Parmesan cheese
1 ½ cups grated cheddar cheese
¼ cup bread crumbs
½ teaspoon salt
¼ teaspoon black pepper

Preheat oven to 350°

Partially steam the broccoli and carrots. Heat oil in a 12-inch frying pan, add hing, stir in tomatoes, and saute for 5 minutes. Add well-rinsed spinach and continue to saute for 3 minutes longer.

In a large bowl combine rice and vegetables. Add ½ teaspoon salt (more may be needed if rice is not already salted). Add remaining ingredients (except ½ cup grated cheese). Do not over-mix. Transfer to a 2-quart casserole dish and top with remaining cheese. Cover and bake for 10 minutes, remove lid, and bake 10 minutes longer. Serve immediately.

Serves 4.

Fruit Juice Gel

2 cups orange juice
2 cups pineapple juice
4 teaspoons agar flakes
1 cup pineapple chunks
1 cup orange sections

Pour the juices into a saucepan and sprinkle in the agar flakes. Allow the agar to soften, about 3 minutes. Bring the juice to a boil, stirring to dissolve the agar. Simmer for 5 minutes.

Pour the juice into a mold or 4 dessert dishes. Refrigerate for 20 minutes or until the juice begins to gel. Stir in the fruit pieces. Chill to set.

Serves 4.

Middle East

Lemon Lentil Soup
Spinach Filo
Eggplant Salad
Stuffed Zucchini
Sweet Pastry

Lemon Lentil Soup

1 cup lentils
6 cups water
1 potato (peeled and cut in ½-inch cubes)
1 cup chopped celery
1 cup chopped Swiss chard
3 tablespoons olive oil
¼ cup chopped coriander leaves
¼ cup chopped parsley leaves
¼ teaspoon hing
½ teaspoon black pepper
1 tablespoon ground coriander
½ teaspoon cumin powder
2 tablespoons lemon juice
salt to taste

Rinse lentils. Bring lentils and water to boil in large pot. Simmer for 35 minutes.

In a separate pan heat oil, add hing, black pepper, and potatoes. Fry for 2 minutes on high heat. Add celery and fry for 1 more minute. Add to lentil broth and cook 10 minutes.

Add Swiss chard, ground coriander, cumin powder, and lemon juice. Cook 10 minutes. Add parsley, coriander leaves, and salt. Serve hot.

Serves 6.

Spinach Filo

2 bunches spinach (washed, chopped, and steamed)
1 cup ricotta cheese
6 ounces feta cheese (crumbled)
½ cup Parmesan cheese
2 tablespoons sour cream
2 teaspoons flour
½ teaspoon nutmeg
½ teaspoon salt (optional)
¼ teaspoon black pepper
¼ cup chopped fresh parsley
1 package filo sheets (thawed)
½ cup melted butter

With wooden spoon beat ricotta, feta, and Parmesan cheeses with sour cream, flour, black pepper, salt, and nutmeg until well mixed. (The cheeses used in this recipe are sometimes salty, so salt may be omitted if you like.) Stir in parsley and spinach.

Cut filo in half, crosswise. Cover it loosely with a damp paper towel to keep it from drying out. With a pastry brush lightly coat the bottom of a 9 x 13-inch baking pan with butter. Line the pan with one sheet of filo, and brush lightly with melted butter. Place another sheet of filo in the pan, and brush with butter. Repeat this until you have used half of the filo.

Spread the spinach-cheese mixture evenly over the filo. Cover with another sheet of filo and brush lightly with butter. Repeat with the remainder of the filo. Cover the top layer with butter. Cover with aluminum foil and refrigerate for at least 2 hours.

Preheat oven to 375°.

Immediately before baking, score top layer of filo with a sharp knife to mark serving-size portions. Bake uncovered for 45 minutes, or until the top is golden. Cool slightly before serving.

Eggplant Salad

2 pounds small eggplants
1/3 cup olive oil
1/4 cup chopped parsley
1/2 teaspoon salt
2 heaping teaspoons minced fresh ginger
2 tablespoons turbinado sugar
2 tablespoons lemon juice

Preheat oven to 400°.

Prick the eggplants with a fork and bake in oven until very tender (about 30 minutes). When they are cool enough to handle, cut in half lengthwise and remove seeds. Scoop the pulp out of the skin and place in a sieve to drain. When the eggplant is well drained put in a large bowl and mash with a wooden spoon. Add the remaining ingredients, mix well, and chill for a few hours.

Serve on a lettuce leaf, surrounded by tomato wedges and olives.

Serves 4.

Stuffed Zucchini

6 medium zucchini (sliced in half lengthwise)
1/4 cup rice
1/2 cup water
2 tablespoons butter
1/4 teaspoon hing
1 stalk celery (chopped)
1 1/2 teaspoons salt
1/4 cup olive oil
1/2 cup bread crumbs
juice of 1 lemon
1 cup Parmesan cheese
1/4 cup chopped parsley

Preheat oven to 350°.

Scoop out insides of zucchinis and set aside.

In a pan melt butter, and add hing and rice. Stir for 1 minute and then add water, salt, and celery. Bring to a boil and then cover, lower heat, and simmer until rice is cooked (about 10 minutes).

Steam the chopped insides of the zucchini for 5 minutes. Add this along with olive oil, bread crumbs, lemon juice, and parsley to the cooked rice.

Place the filling into the zucchini shells. Arrange the shells in a shallow baking dish. Sprinkle with Parmesan cheese. Cover the pan with aluminum foil and bake for approximately 30 minutes. Remove the cover and bake 8 minutes longer, or until cheese begins to brown.

Serves 4.

Sweet Pastry

Filling:

6 cups milk
½ cup toasted coconut
½ teaspoon vanilla
⅓ cup turbinado sugar
1 teaspoon cornstarch

Dough:

1 cup flour
2 teaspoons turbinado sugar
1 tablespoon heavy cream
1 ½ tablespoons melted butter
¼ cup plus 1 tablespoon water

Glaze:

3 tablespoons honey
¼ cup chopped pistachio nuts
ghee or oil for deep frying

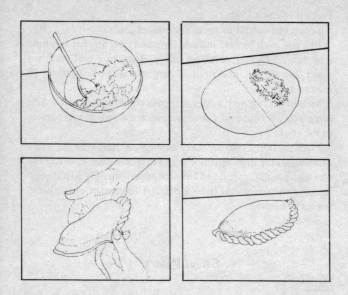

Using milk, make curd (see recipe, page 80), and press it for 10 minutes.

Mix together curd, toasted coconut, vanilla, sugar, and cornstarch. Set aside.

In another bowl combine flour, sugar, cream, melted butter, and water. Knead for 5 minutes.

Heat ghee or oil in wok.

Divide dough into eight balls. Roll out each ball into a 5-inch circle and place 3 tablespoons stuffing in the center. Fold over and press. Seal edges to form loops.

Fry in medium-hot ghee for about 15 minutes, turning occasionally until both sides are golden brown. Remove from ghee and drain on paper towels.

Glaze each sweet with a little honey and sprinkle with chopped nuts. Serve warm or cool.

Makes 8.

Vegetables

Stuffed Peppers
Upma
Cauliflower, Pea Pods, and Cashews
Asparagus Casserole
Mixed Vegetable Curry
Fried Eggplant Slices
Gouranga Potatoes
Cauliflower Parmesan
Potato "Omelet"
Creamed Spinach and Cauliflower

Stuffed Peppers

4 large green peppers
1 ½ cups cooked rice (salted)
⅓ cup oil or ghee
¼ teaspoon hing
1 ½ teaspoons fennel seeds
1 teaspoon black pepper
1 cup chopped zucchini
½ cup chopped black olives
⅓ cup pine nuts
1 teaspoon salt
1 cup ricotta cheese
½ cup Parmesan cheese

Cut tops off peppers, remove seeds, and steam peppers until tender (about 10 minutes).

In skillet heat 1 tablespoon oil, and add hing, fennel seeds, and black pepper. Fry until fennel seeds turn golden. Add zucchini and fry on medium heat for 8 minutes. Add olives and pine nuts. Fry for 3 more minutes, then add ricotta cheese and salt. Fry 1 more minute, and remove from heat. Add rice to fried mixture, and stir well. Spoon stuffing into peppers.

Heat remaining ghee or oil in skillet. Fry peppers until golden on all sides. Turn carefully so as not to let stuffing fall out. Sprinkle with Parmesan cheese. Serve hot.

Serves 4.

Upma

½ pound brussels sprouts (cut in half)
4 medium ripe tomatoes (chopped)
1 cup peas
1 zucchini (cut in ½-inch cubes)
1 cup chopped spinach
⅔ cup semolina
4 tablespoons ghee
1 ½ teaspoons salt
1 teaspoon oregano flakes
1 teaspoon basil leaves
1 tablespoon ground coriander
¼ teaspoon black pepper
pinch of hing

In skillet heat ghee. Add hing, chopped tomatoes, brussels sprouts, and zucchini. Cover and fry on medium heat for 15 minutes. Add peas, spinach, and spices. Cover and cook for an additional 5 minutes. Remove cover and gradually stir in semolina. Stir on low heat until liquid is absorbed by semolina (about 1 minute). Remove from heat, cover and let stand for 5 minutes before serving.

Serves 4.

Cauliflower, Pea Pods, and Cashews

3 cups cauliflower (cut in flowerets)
1 cup Chinese pea pods (remove ends)
½ cup whole cashews
1 cup sour cream
1 teaspoon salt
½ teaspoon black pepper
pinch of turmeric
pinch of hing

In wok, deep fry cauliflower pieces over medium-hot heat until golden and tender.

Put cashews in a small strainer and dip in hot ghee for about 10 seconds until golden. Strain.

Steam pea pods for 3 minutes.

Combine pea pods, cauliflower, cashews, and sour cream. Add spices. Heat in saucepan for 1 minute. Serve hot.

Serves 4.

Asparagus Casserole

2 pounds asparagus (cut into diagonal slices)
1 cup cherry tomatoes
½ cup butter
1 ½ cups milk
½ cup evaporated milk
⅓ cup flour
½ teaspoon curry powder
pinch of hing
1 teaspoon salt
1 teaspoon black pepper
⅓ cup grated Romano cheese
¼ cup grated monterrey jack cheese

Steam asparagus until tender. Drain.

Preheat oven to 400°.

In saucepan melt butter, add hing, black pepper, and curry. Add flour and both kinds of milk. Cook over low heat until mixture thickens.

In casserole dish combine asparagus, cherry tomatoes, milk sauce, cheeses, and salt. Bake uncovered for 20 minutes. Garnish with parsley.

Serves 4.

Mixed Vegetable Curry

2 cups broccoli (cut in small flowerets)
1 large potato (peeled and cut in ¾-inch cubes)
2 carrots (cut in ⅓-inch slices)
½ cup sour cream
1 cup milk
2 tablespoons flour
½ teaspoon turmeric
1 teaspoon cumin powder
1 tablespoon coriander powder
pinch of hing
1 ½ teaspoons salt
ghee for deep frying

Steam broccoli until tender. Deep fry potatoes on high heat until golden and tender. Then deep fry carrots until golden and tender. Drain and set aside vegetables.

In small saucepan put 1 tablespoon ghee and add flour and milk. Bring to a boil and cook until mixture thickens. Add all spices except salt and cook 30 seconds more. Then stir in sour cream and salt. Mix vegetables into sauce. Serve hot.

Serves 4.

Fried Eggplant Slices

1 large eggplant
3 teaspoons turmeric
1 teaspoon salt
4 teaspoons water
ghee for deep frying

Cut eggplant in 1-inch-thick circles. Cut each circle in half.

Heat ghee to very hot temperature.

Mix turmeric, salt, and water. Rub mixture into both sides of eggplant slices. Deep fry eggplant pieces until dark, golden, and crisp. Drain on paper towels and serve hot.

Serves 4.

Gouranga Potatoes

8 medium potatoes
½ cup melted butter
2 cups sour cream
1 teaspoon turmeric
2 teaspoons salt
¼ teaspoon hing
½ teaspoon ground rosemary
1 teaspoon black pepper
1 teaspoon paprika

In large saucepan parboil potatoes. Drain and refrigerate. When potatoes are cooled, peel and cut in ½-inch slices.

Preheat oven to 400°.

In bowl combine sour cream, butter, and spices. Add potatoes to sour-cream mixture. Stir gently and place in casserole dish. Cover and bake 25 minutes. Serve hot.

Serves 4.

Cauliflower Parmesan

2 medium cauliflower (cut in flowerets)
2 cups tomato puree
¼ cup water
2 cups grated mozzarella cheese
1 cup bread crumbs
¼ cup Parmesan cheese
2 teaspoons salt
2 tablespoons olive oil
1 tablespoon sweet basil
1 teaspoon black pepper
pinch of hing
ghee for deep frying

Deep fry cauliflower flowerets in hot ghee until golden and tender. Drain and set aside.

In skillet heat olive oil, and add hing and black pepper. Add bread crumbs and fry for 2 minutes. Add tomato puree, water, and sweet basil. Cover and cook for 15 minutes on medium heat, stirring occasionally.

Stir cauliflower pieces into sauce. Cover with grated mozzarella cheese. Do not stir. Cover and simmer for 4 minutes. Sprinkle with Parmesan cheese. Serve hot.

Serves 4.

Potato "Omelet"

6 medium red or white potatoes
8 teaspoons ghee or oil
salt
pepper
turmeric
hing
2 tomatoes (thinly sliced)
8 large spinach leaves
½ pound cheddar or monterrey jack cheese (grated)

Grate potatoes and place in a bowl of cold water. In 8-inch nonstick or wrought-iron frying pan heat 1 teaspoon ghee over medium heat. Take a handful of grated potatoes, squeeze out the excess water, and spread evenly on the bottom of the pan. Sprinkle a pinch each of salt, pepper, turmeric, and hing evenly over the potatoes. Cover and cook on low heat until the potatoes are tender and hold together. Flip the "omelet" over, cover, and cook for 2 minutes longer until bottom is golden brown.

Cover half of the "omelet" with some sliced tomatoes, grated cheese, and a spinach leaf. Fold in half and fry until the cheese begins to melt and the tomato and spinach soften. Remove from heat and place on a baking sheet. Place in warm oven while you continue making the remaining "omelets." Serve warm.

Serves 4.

Creamed Spinach and Cauliflower

½ cup butter
4 cups chopped spinach
1 cup cauliflower (cut into small flowerets)
6 ounces cream cheese
1 teaspoon salt
½ teaspoon black pepper
pinch of hing

In skillet heat butter on low heat. When melted add black pepper, hing, and cauliflower and fry on medium heat for 6 minutes. Add spinach and fry on medium heat for 15 minutes. Turn heat off when all moisture is absorbed. Add salt and cream cheese. Stir and serve hot.

Serves 4.

Miscellaneous Side Dishes

Tostadas
Pita Pizza
Bharats in Yogurt Sauce
Stuffed Parathas
Banana Vadis
Potato-and-Pea Croquettes
Curd Patties
Scrambled-Pepper-and-Curd Hero
Vegetarian Nutloaf

Tostadas

6 corn tortillas
2 cups cooked pinto beans
2 tablespoons butter
¼ teaspoon hing
1 tablespoon chili powder
½ teaspoon cumin powder
¼ cup water
oil for deep frying

Garnishings:

shredded lettuce
thin tomato wedges
sliced black olives
grated cheddar cheese
sour cream
Mexican Hot Sauce (recipe follows)

Fry tortillas in very hot oil until crispy and lightly browned. Drain on paper towel and set aside.

In skillet heat butter. Add hing and chili powder. Stir in beans and cumin powder, and mash to a thick paste. Later you may need to add a little water to keep the paste spreadable.

Spread refried beans on fried tortilla and top with garnishings.

Mexican Hot Sauce:

¼ teaspoon hing
1 teaspoon minced green chili
1 tablespoon oil
1 teaspoon chili powder
½ teaspoon lemon juice
1 cup tomato puree
½ teaspoon salt
pinch of turbinado sugar

Heat oil in pan, and add hing and green chili. Fry until chili begins to brown. Add chili powder, lemon juice, and tomato puree. Simmer uncovered for 5 minutes, or until slightly thickened. Add salt and sugar.

Pita Pizza

4 7-inch whole wheat pita breads
2 cups sliced zucchini
1 cup sliced black olives
1 cup chopped green peppers
1 ½ cups grated mozzarella cheese
1 ½ cups grated monterrey jack cheese
¼ cup Parmesan cheese
oregano
Tomato Sauce (recipe follows)

Preheat oven to 500°.

Place 2 pita breads on baking sheet. Spread each with ¼ of tomato sauce. Top with vegetables and cheese. Sprinkle with oregano. Bake 15 minutes or until the cheese begins to bubble and brown. Repeat with remaining pita breads.

Tomato Sauce:

1 ½ cups tomato puree
¼ cup water
2 tablespoons olive oil
¼ teaspoon hing
1 teaspoon sweet basil
1 teaspoon salt
1 teaspoon oregano

In saucepan heat olive oil over medium heat. Add hing and basil, and stir in puree, water, and salt. Cover and bring to a boil, reduce heat, and simmer for 15 minutes, stirring occasionally. Remove from heat and stir in oregano.

Bharats in Yogurt Sauce

1 ½ cups green split peas (soaked in water overnight)
2 cups yogurt
½ cup sour cream
½ cup water
1 ½ teaspoons salt
1 teaspoon ground coriander
1 teaspoon cumin powder
1 teaspoon garam masala
pinch of hing
pinch of cayenne
½ teaspoon turmeric
ghee for deep frying

Drain beans and grind in blender or food processor, adding a few tablespoons of water. Add spices and mix.

Heat ghee in wok until very hot. Mold ground bean mixture into 3-inch patties. Gently place patties in hot ghee and cook until dark golden brown (about 10 minutes). Do not stir bharats immediately. Let them first cook for 2 minutes, or until firm, before stirring. Drain and set in casserole dish.

Preheat oven to 375°.

In bowl combine yogurt, sour cream, and water. Pour mixture over bharats. Cover and bake in oven for 8 minutes. Serve hot, garnished with parsley.

Serves 4.

Stuffed Parathas

Filling:

½ gallon milk
1 bunch spinach (chopped)
1 medium tomato (cut in 16 pieces)
2 tablespoons ghee
pinch of hing
1 tablespoon mustard seeds
pinch of turmeric
½ teaspoon salt
¼ teaspoon black pepper
2 cups ghee for frying

From milk, make curd (see recipe, page 80). Curd does not have to be pressed for this preparation but should sit in colander for 10 minutes and drain.

Heat ghee in a nonstick skillet, and add mustard seeds. When they begin to crackle add hing and turmeric. Add tomatoes and stir fry for 2 minutes. Add spinach and fry for 5 minutes longer. Add curd, salt, and pepper, and fry for 5 more minutes or until all liquid has evaporated. Set aside and cool.

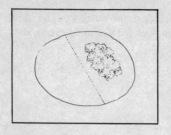

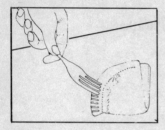

Dough:

1 ½ cups white flour
1 ½ cups whole wheat flour
¼ teaspoon salt
½ cup ghee
¾ cup water

Combine flours and salt, mix in ghee, and then add water until mixture is a rollable dough. Knead for 5 minutes.

Divide dough into 12 balls and roll each ball into a circle 5 inches in diameter. Place 3 tablespoons stuffing on half of the circle, making sure it is not too close to the edges. Fold the circle in half, pressing edges together. Carefully pat down to remove any air bubbles. Again fold the dough in half and press edges together. You will have what resembles a triangle.

Heat ghee in skillet. Place 4 parathas in the pan at a time. Fry on each side on medium heat for about 3 minutes. They will be reddish golden.

Serve warm—plain or with a chutney.

Makes 1 dozen.

Banana Vadis

2 large, unripened green bananas
1 tablespoon ground pistachio nuts
2 tablespoons blanched and ground almonds
2 tablespoons raisins (soaked in hot water)
¼ cup flour
1 tablespoon garam masala
½ teaspoon salt
pinch of hing
¼ teaspoon grated fresh ginger
½ small green chili (minced)
2 cups yogurt
2 cups ghee

Boil green bananas until skins pop open. Drain and cool, then peel and mash. Add flour, salt, hing, grated ginger, and chili.

Mash together raisins and ground nuts. Make 12 pellet-size balls with this fruit-and-nut combination.

Now make 12 2-inch balls with the banana mixture. With your index finger, make an indention in a banana ball and place a fruit-and-nut pellet in it. Mold banana mixture around pellet. Then in the palm of your hand form each ball into an oval shape.

Heat ghee in skillet over medium heat. When hot add stuffed banana vadis and fry for 4 minutes on each side or until golden brown. Drain and put in serving dish. Cover with yogurt and sprinkle with garam masala. Serve cold.

Makes 1 dozen.

Potato-and-Pea Croquettes

3 medium large potatoes (peeled and cut in ½-inch cubes)
1 cup peas
¼ cup minced fresh coriander leaves (or parsley)
1 cup bread crumbs
1 teaspoon salt
1 teaspoon black pepper
1 cup sour cream
¼ cup ghee or oil for frying

Boil potatoes in saucepan until very tender. Mash and set aside. Steam peas and set aside.

Add spices and bread crumbs to mashed potatoes. Then add peas. Divide the mixture into 12 3-inch balls. Flatten each ball in the palms of your hands to make into patties.

In nonstick skillet heat ½ of the ghee. Fry 6 of the patties on both sides until golden (about 3 minutes on each side).

Add remaining ghee and fry remaining 6 patties.

Serve hot, with sour cream on the side.

Makes 1 dozen.

Curd Patties

1 gallon milk
2 teaspoons salt
1 tablespoon chopped fresh coriander leaves
4 tablespoons ghee
½ teaspoon black pepper

From milk, make curd (see recipe, page 80). Press curd for 20 minutes. Knead curd into a smooth consistency by pressing against counter top or board with palm of hand.

Add coriander leaves and spices to curd. Make 12 balls and form into patties 2 inches in diameter.

Heat ghee in nonstick skillet over medium heat. Fry patties on both sides until golden brown (about 5 minutes).

Serve hot—plain or with tomato chutney.

Makes 1 dozen.

Scrambled-Pepper-and-Curd Hero

3 quarts milk
2 large green peppers (sliced into 1-inch strips)
4 6-inch French breads
3 tablespoons olive oil
¾ teaspoon salt
pinch of hing
pinch of turmeric
pinch of black pepper

From milk, make curd (see recipe, page 80). Do not press curd. Drain in colander for 10 minutes.

In skillet heat 3 tablespoons olive oil. Add hing and pepper strips. Fry over high heat until peppers are tender and brownish (about 8 minutes). Reduce heat. Add salt, turmeric, and curd. Fry for 5 more minutes.

Preheat oven to 450°.

Slice French breads (not all the way through). Heat in oven for 1 minute. Evenly divide pepper-and-curd mixture on breads. Serve hot.

Makes 4 heros.

Vegetarian Nutloaf

⅓ cup chopped celery
⅓ cup chopped green pepper
½ cup walnuts
½ cup cashews
½ cup almonds (blanched)
1 ¾ cups cooked rice
1 ½ cups grated monterrey jack cheese
1 tablespoon sage
½ tablespoon thyme
1 teaspoon basil
½ tablespoon salt
¼ teaspoon hing
1 teaspoon black pepper
1 ½ cups Tomato Sauce (recipe follows)

Grind nuts together. Combine ground nuts and rice. Add 1 cup grated cheese. Add spices and chopped vegetables. Add ½ cup tomato sauce. Mix well.

Preheat oven to 350°.

Mold ingredients into a greased loaf pan.

Cover with aluminum foil and bake for 50 minutes. Uncover and top with remaining tomato sauce and cheese. Bake for 10 more minutes. Serve hot.

Tomato Sauce:

1 small can tomato puree (8 ounces)
¼ cup oil or ghee
1 teaspoon black pepper
pinch of hing
1 teaspoon salt
1 tablespoon basil leaves
pinch of sugar

In 1-quart saucepan add ghee. When hot add black pepper and hing. Quickly add tomato puree. Add ½ cup water, pinch of sugar, salt, and basil leaves. Cook on medium heat for ½ hour, stirring often.

Serves 4.

Hare Kṛṣṇa Food for Life distributes nutritious free vegetarian food to the hungry in twenty-five cities throughout America.

══════ Appendix ══════

Hare Kṛṣṇa Food for Life

The International Society for Krishna Consciousness is doing a superb job of letting people know that vegetarian food is healthful, delicious, and pleasing to the eye. Over the past fifteen years the Hare Krishna people have distributed more than 150 million plates of prasadam, vegetarian foods prepared and offered to God with love and devotion. They are master cooks, their food is stunningly delicious, and they cannot be praised enough for their success in promoting the cause of vegetarianism worldwide.

—Scott Smith, Associate Editor
Vegetarian Times

The careful preparation and profuse public distribution of *prasādam* (vegetarian foods offered to Lord Kṛṣṇa) has always been an essential element of the Vedic culture. Since 1966, devotees of the International Society for Krishna Consciousness (ISKCON) have followed this tradition by serving out over 150 million nourishing free multicourse dinners, opening over thirty vegetarian restaurants, founding over thirty vegetarian farm communities, providing vegetarian food relief to the hungry in

Asia, Africa, and the West, and widely publicizing the value of a spiritual vegetarian diet through books, magazines, and films. Also, many followers of the Kṛṣṇa religion have begun various *prasādam* businesses, producing a wide variety of healthy, nutritious, natural foods. All this makes the International Society for Krishna Consciousness—unique in its spiritual approach to diet—the strongest and most well-organized force for vegetarianism in the world today.

Free Sunday Feast

The founder-*ācārya* (spiritual master) of the Hare Kṛṣṇa movement, Śrīla Prabhupāda, started the now-famous Sunday feasts in 1966. At the first Kṛṣṇa temple in the Western world, located in New York's Lower East Side, he would personally help cook the twelve-course meals. Regular attendance at the feast rapidly increased to three or four hundred people. Generally these feasts consisted of:

- *puris*—a light tortillalike whole wheat bread fried in ghee (clarified butter).
- *pushpanna rice*—an opulent rice dish, prepared with nuts and spices.
- *samosas*—a fried pastry stuffed with cauliflower and peas.
- *pakoras*—vegetables dipped in chick-pea batter and deep-fried in ghee.
- two or more *subjis*—cooked vegetables, often including small cubes of fresh, homemade cheese.
- *kheer*—a dessert of sweetened condensed milk.
- *burfi*—a milk sweet resembling vanilla fudge.
- *lassi*—cooling yogurt-fruit drinks.

In 1967 Hare Kṛṣṇa devotees opened their second temple, in San Francisco's Haight-Ashbury district, where they served *prasādam* meals free to over 250 people daily. By the early 1970s, the ISKCON Sunday feast had been established as a weekly event in major cities throughout the world, including New York, Boston, Washington, D.C., San Francisco, Los Angeles, San Diego, Mexico City, Montreal, London, Paris, Rome, Amsterdam, Frankfurt, Nairobi, Calcutta, Bombay, Sydney, Melbourne, and Rio de Janeiro. Śrīla Prabhupāda often light-heartedly referred to the Hare Kṛṣṇa movement as "the kitchen religion," thus expressing his satisfaction with how well his followers were carrying out his desire to flood the world with *prasādam*.

Festivals

In addition to serving *prasādam* each Sunday at ISKCON temples, devotees also began to bring their spiritual vegetarian food out to the public in a variety of ways. Ever since the days of Woodstock, devotees have set up *prasādam* kitchens at outdoor gatherings to provide sumptuous free vegetarian food. Recently devotees have served thousands of plates of *prasādam* at events such as the California US Festival, the Glastonbury Festival near Stonehenge, England, the New Zealand Sweetwaters festival, large-scale national peace rallies in Western Germany, and cultural festivals throughout Central and South America. ISKCON members regularly set up *prasādam* booths at fairs and health- or food-related conventions. The Hare Kṛṣṇa movement also stages its own massive festivals, such as Ratha-yātrā (the Festival of the Chariots), held annually in Los Angeles, Boston, New York, Washington, D.C., Montreal, Toronto, New

Orleans, Sydney, Melbourne, London, Bombay, and other major cities throughout the world. At each event, devotees distribute tens of thousands of plates of delicious vegetarian food. Scott Smith, associate editor of the *Vegetarian Times,* recently remarked, "The Hare Kṛṣṇa cooks are the only mass preparers of foodstuffs who maintain such an extraordinarily and consistently high quality of culinary excellence, even when catering to as many as twelve thousand people at a go." When members of ISKCON's Los Angeles center catered a vegetarian luncheon at a celebrity tennis tournament for the National Kidney Foundation, the tournament chairman wrote that the food's "tastiness and healthfulness was all excellent."

Celebrities Enjoy *Prasādam*

Over the past few years, devotees of Kṛṣṇa have appeared in over two dozen feature films and network television dramas. The chanting of Hare Kṛṣṇa has also been recorded by many top musicians on their albums. These events afforded ISKCON members the opportunity to share delicious *prasādam* meals with many of the entertainment industry's brightest stars, all of whom deeply appreciated their experiences with the delicious spiritual vegetarian foods. These include Dustin Hoffman, Muhammad Ali, Sally Struthers, Stevie Wonder, Ed Asner, Steve Allen, Elliot Gould, Richie Havens, Dick Gregory, Julie Christie, George Harrison, Ringo Starr, John Lennon, Paul and Linda McCartney, Marsha Mason, Bob Dylan, Jerry Garcia and other members of the Grateful Dead, Ray Harryhausen, Jackson Browne, Gordon (Sting) Sumner of the Police, Ray Davies of the Kinks, and many others. In a 1982 interview, George Harrison said of *prasādam*, "I think it's great. It's a pity you don't have restaurants or temples on all the main streets of every little town and village like those hamburger and fried chicken places. You should put them out of business."

Restaurants

By the early 1980s, members of the Hare Kṛṣṇa movement had opened restaurants in places such as Paris, London, Bombay, Melbourne, Sydney, New York, San Francisco, San Diego, Toronto, Montreal, and at Prabhupāda's Palace of Gold in West Virginia. Each restaurant had built up a steady, satisfied clientele, and restaurant reviewers had given unqualified praise in leading magazines and newspapers. Liz Logan of the *Dallas News* says of the movement's Dallas restaurant: "Pleasant surprises are so much nicer than the other kind. And Kalachandji's is a pleasant—no, make that wonderful—surprise. Located in far East Dallas, the Hare Kṛṣṇa-operated restaurant serves a $5.50 *prix fixe* Vedic dinner five nights a week. (Vedic cuisine translates to vegetarian, Indian fare.) For the price and the food, this may be the best bargain in town. . . . As if this generally astonishing food were not enough, Kalachandji's setting also astonishes. The indoor seating is pleasant enough, but the outdoor courtyard is the real attraction."

Of Govinda's Natural Foods Restaurant in Los Angeles, a reviewer for *Los Angeles* magazine said, "They cook very well and have an enthusiastic following of customers." Marveling at the stunning decor of the restaurant at the Hare Kṛṣṇa movement's Detroit cultural center, originally built by Cadillac founder Lawrence P. ("Body by") Fisher, *People* magazine said, "Tourists dine at Govinda's, a gourmet vegetarian restaurant whose opulent marble-and-onyx decor makes Manhattan's legendary Russian Tea Room look like an interstate truck stop." The food served there lives up to the surroundings. The devotee cooks in the restaurants of the Hare Kṛṣṇa movement follow the Vedic tradition of preparing an endless variety of exotic dishes fit for kings and queens. Suzanne Moore of *Diet Times* wrote, "A feast of food, a feast of culture, and a feast of happiness. They lovingly prepare and serve an amazing array of Indian vegetarian dishes. And what a spread—it makes the Taj Mahal look plain."

Although all ISKCON restaurants strive to offer their clientele a sublime atmosphere for dining, their main business is to provide high quality, healthful, delicious *prasādam* at a cost everyone can afford. The Cleveland city council passed this resolution in praise of the Hare Kṛṣṇa movement's restaurant there: "Whereas Govinda's is a benefit for the poor, for the elderly, men and women, black and white; and whereas Govinda's presence is greatly appreciated by the masses of this community . . . this council wishes to express its most heartfelt appreciation for the selfless effort of the International Society for Krishna Consciousness for their many services to the community."

Farm Communities

Śrīla Prabhupāda often stated that the world's economic problems—including the food problem—could be easily solved if people simply depended upon the land and the cows. The cow supplies ample milk, butter, cheese, and yogurt, and by using the bull one can plow the fields and produce abundant grains and vegetables. From the forest one can obtain honey, nuts, and fruits. To practically demonstrate this simple truth, Śrīla Prabhupāda organized Vedic farm communities, over thirty of which are now flourishing around the world. Visitors can taste wonderful *prasādam* meals prepared from healthful, natural vegetarian ingredients produced right on the farms themselves.

International Food Relief

"No one within ten miles of our temples should go hungry," Śrīla Prabhupāda once told his disciples. This compassionate concern for the undernourished led to the establishment of ISKCON Food Relief, which for the past ten years has provided *prasādam* to hundreds of thousands of hungry people in Asia and Africa. In 1977 one of the biggest floods in recent history inundated West Bengal. Hare Kṛṣṇa members on the scene immediately went into action. Risking their lives, they traveled in small boats equipped with outboard motors over hundreds of miles of dangerously raging floodwaters to procure staples such as rice and *dāl*. They then cooked these ingredients on the rooftop of their own flooded *āśrama* building and transported the food by the boatload to isolated villages, saving thousands from starvation. Recently ISKCON members have been working with CARE and Indian local governments in a joint program (the West Bengal Council for Child Welfare's Mother-Child Nutritional Health Program). Over 360,000 plates of nutritious Hare Kṛṣṇa *prasādam* have been distributed in this massive effort. CARE official R. K. Narula stated that the ISKCON distribution centers "are being run very efficiently."

In the West, the Hare Kṛṣṇa movement has been distributing free *prasādam* meals to the unemployed and others living below the poverty level through its Hare Kṛṣṇa

Food for Life program. In America, Hare Kṛṣṇa Food for Life currently feeds thousands of people each week in twenty-five cities. Elizabeth Reuther (Lekhāśravantī dāsī), daughter of Walter Reuther, the late United Auto Workers labor union president, and now an ISKCON member, helped launch Food for Life in Detroit.

Publicity

Through its different cookbooks, including *The Higher Taste*, the Hare Kṛṣṇa movement has introduced the philosophy and preparation of *prasādam* to millions of people throughout the world. Devotees also distribute millions of copies of the most essential books of Vedic knowledge, such as *Bhagavad-gītā*, *Śrīmad-Bhāgavatam,* and *Caitanya-caritāmṛta*, which fully explain the law of *karma*, the doctrine of *ahiṁsā* (nonviolence), and other foundations of a truly spiritual approach to vegetarianism. Information about *prasādam* is also being disseminated through radio, television, and film media, and devotees hold vegetarian cooking classes at ISKCON temples and restaurants, at colleges and universities, and at private homes.

ISKCON Centers
Around the World

NORTH AMERICA

CANADA

Calgary, Alberta—10516 Oakfield Dr., S.W. Calgary T2W 2A9 / (403) 238-0602
Edmonton, Alberta—8957 77th Ave., T5N 2N7 / (403) 466-5119
Halifax, Nova Scotia—2350 Agricola St., B3K 4B6 / (902) 423-4607
Montreal, Quebec—1626 Pie IX Blvd., H1V 2C5 / (514) 527-1101
Montreal, Quebec—537A Ste. Catherine West, H3B 1B2 / (514) 845-2010
Ottawa, Ontario—212 Somerset St. E., K1N 6V4 / (613) 233-1884
Regina, Saskatchewan—2817 Victoria Ave., S4T 1K6 / (306) 522-4973
Toronto, Ontario—243 Avenue Rd., M5R 2J6 / (416) 922-5415
Vancouver, B.C.—5462 S.E. Marine Dr., Burnaby V5J 3G8 / (604) 433-9728

FARMS

Ashcroft, B.C. (Śaraṇāgati-dhāma)—Box 1417, V0K 1A0

RESTAURANTS

Montreal—Chez Govinda, 3678 Saint Denis St. / (514) 843-8510
Ottawa—The Back Home Buffet, 212 Somerset St. E. / (613) 233-3460

U.S.A.

Ann Arbor, MI—606 Packard St., 48104 / (313) 665-9057
Athens, OH—89 Mill St., 45701 / (614) 592-4740
Atlanta, GA—1287 Ponce de Leon Ave. N.E., 30306 / (404) 377-8680
Baltimore, MD—200 Bloomsbury Ave., Catonsville, 21228 / (301) 788-3885
Boston, MA—72 Commonwealth Ave., 02116 / (617) 247-8611
Boulder, CO—917 Pleasant St., 80302 / (303) 344-7005
Caguas, PR—Calle Ruiz Belvis No. 42, 00625 / (809) 746-9829
Chicago, IL—1716 W. Lunt Ave., 60626 (312) 973-0900
Cleveland, OH—15720 Euclid Ave., E. Cleveland, 44112 / (216) 681-3193
Columbus, OH—379 W. 8th Ave., 43201 /(614) 421-1661
Dallas, TX—5430 Gurley Ave., 75223 / (214) 827-6330
Denver, CO—1400 Cherry St., 80220 / (303) 333-5461
Detroit, MI—383 Lenox Ave., 48215 / (313) 824-6000
Fullerton, CA—2011 E. Chapman Ave., 92631 / (714) 870-1156
Gurabo, PR—Rt. 181, Box 215-B, Santa Rita, 00658 / (809) 763-9312
Hartford, Ct—1683 Main St., E. Hartford, 06108 / (203) 289-7252
Honolulu, HI—51 Coelho Way, 96817 / (808) 595-3947
Houston, TX—1111 Rosalie St., (mail: P.O. Box 2927, 77252) / (713) 526-9860
Laguna Beach, CA—285 Legion St., 92651 / (714) 494-7029
Lake Huntington, NY—P.O. Box 388, 12752 / (914) 932-8273
Long Island, NY—197 S. Ocean Ave., Freeport, 11520 / (516) 378-6184
Los Angeles, CA—3764 Watseka Ave., 90034 / (213) 836-2676
Miami Beach, FL—2445 Collins Ave., 33140 / (305) 531-0331
Morgantown, WV—322 Beverly Ave., 26505 / (304) 292-6725
New Orleans, LA—2936 Esplanade Ave., 70119 / (504) 488-7433
New York, NY—305 Schermerhorn St., Brooklyn, 11217 / (718) 855-6714
New York, NY—46 Greenwich, Manhattan 10011 / (212) 924-8083
Philadelphia, PA—51 W. Allens Lane, 19119 / (215) 247-4600
Providence, RI—39 Glendale Ave., 02906 / (401) 273-9010
Spanish Fork, UT—KHQN Radio 1480, 8618 S. Hwy 6 (mail: P.O. Box 379, 84600) / (801) 798-3559
St. Louis, MO—3926 Lindell Blvd., 63108 / (314) 535-8085
San Diego, CA—1030 Grand Ave., Pacific Beach, 92109 / (619) 483-2500
San Francisco, CA—84 Carl St., 94117 / (415) 753-8647
Seattle, WA—3114 E. Pine St., 98122 / (206) 329-7011
State College, PA—103 E. Hamilton Ave., 16801 / (814) 234-1867
Tallahassee, FL—1323 Nylic St. (mail: P.O. Box 20224, 32304) / (904) 681-9258
Tampa, FL—2506 Azeele St., 33606 / (813) 872-6694
Topanga, CA—20395 Callon Dr., 90290 ·/ (213) 455-1658
Towaco, NJ—(mail: P.O. Box 109, 07082) / (201) 299-0970
Washington, D.C.—10310 Oaklyn Rd., Potomac, MD, 20854 / (301) 299-2100
Washington, D.C.—2128 O St. N.W., 20037 / (202) 293-0825

FARMS
Caddo, OK (New Kurukṣetra)—Rt. 1, Box 296, 74729 / (405) 367-2331
Carriere, MS (New Talavan)—Rt. 2, Box 449, 39426 / (601) 798-8533
Gainesville, FL (New Ramaṇa-reti)—Rt. 2, Box 24, Alachua, 32615 / (904) 462-9046
Gurabo, PR (New Govardhana Hill)—(contact ISKCON Gurabo)
Hillsborough, NC (New Goloka)—Rt. 6, Box 701, 27278 / (919) 732-6492
Mulberry, TN (Murāri-sevaka)—Murari Project, Rt. 1, Box 146-A, 37359 / (615) 759-7331
New Vrindaban, WV—R.D. 1, Box 319, Hare Krishna Ridge, 26041 / (304) 843-1600
Ninole, HI (New Kṛṣṇaloka)—P.O. Box 108, 96773 / (808) 595-3947
Philo, CA (Gaura-maṇḍala-giri)—P.O. Box 179, 95466 / (707) 895-2300
Port Royal, PA (Gītā-nāgari)—R.D. 1, Box 163, 17082 / (717) 527-4101
Roadhouse, IL (New Amṛta-deśa)—Rt. 1, Box 70, 62082 (contact ISKCON St. Louis) / (314) 535-8085
Three Rivers, CA (Bhaktivedanta Village)—44799 Dinely Dr., 93271 / (209) 561-3302
RESTAURANTS
Dallas—Kalachandji's (at ISKCON Dallas)
Detroit—Govinda's (at ISKCON Detroit) / (313) 331-6740
Los Angeles—Govinda's, 9624 Venice Blvd., Culver City, 90230 / (213) 836-1269
New Orleans—Govinda's, 1309 Decatur St., 70116 / (504) 522-3538
New Vrindaban—Palace of Gold Restaurant / (304) 843-1233 (open May–Nov.)
St. Louis—Govinda's (at ISKCON St. Louis) / (314) 535-8085
San Diego—Govinda's, 3012 University Ave., North Park, 92104 / (619) 284-4827
San Francisco—Jagannatha's Cart, 57 Jessie St., 94105 / (415) 495-3083
San Juan—Govinda's, Tetuan 153, Viejo, 00903 / (809) 727-4885

EUROPE
ENGLAND AND IRELAND
Belfast, Northern Ireland—23 Wellington Park, Malone Rd., BT9 6DL / 668-874
Dublin, Ireland—6 Dawson Lane (off Dawson St.), Dublin 2
Dublin, Ireland—Castlefield House, Knocklyn Road, Temple Logue, Dublin 16 / 945-504
London, England (city)—10 Soho St., London W1 / (1) 437-8442
London, England (country)—Bhaktivedanta Manor, Letchmore Heath, Watford, Hertsfordshire WD2 8EP / (9276) 7244
FARMS
Glengariff, Ireland (Hare Kṛṣṇa Farm)—County Cork
London, England—(contact Bhaktivedanta Manor)
RESTAURANTS
London—Govinda's, 9–10 Soho St. / (1) 437-8442
ITALY
Bologna—Via Saliceto 1, 40013 Castelmaggiore (BO) / (51) 700-868
Catania—Via San Nicolo al Borgo 28, 95128 Catania, Sicily / (95) 552-252
Naples—Via Torricelli 77, 80059 Torre Del Greco (NA) / (81) 881-5431
Padua—Via delle Granze 107, 35040 Loc. Camin (PD) / (49) 760-007
Pisa—Via delle Colline, Loc. La Meridiana, 56030 Perignano (PI) / (587) 616-194
Rome—Via di Tor Tre Teste 142, 00169 Roma / (6) 263-157
Turin—Strada Berra 19, 1, Loc. Tetti Gariglio, 10025 Pino Torinese (TO) / (11) 840-957
Varese—Via Volta 19, 21013 Gallarate (Va) / (331) 783-268
FARM
Florence, Italy (Villa Vṛndāvana)—Via Communale degli Scopeti 108, S. Andrea in Percussina, 50026 San Casciano Val.di Pesa (FI) / (55) 820-054
RESTAURANTS
Milan—Govinda's, Via Valpetrosa 3/5, 20123 Milano / (2) 862-417
Rome—Via di San Simone 73/A, 00186 Roma / (6) 654-8856
OTHER COUNTRIES
Amsterdam, Holland—Keizersgracht 94 / (20) 24-94-10
Athens, Greece—Bhaktivedanta Cultural Assoc., 133 Solonos / (1) 364-1618
Bergen, Norway—Storhaugen 6, 5000 Bergen / (5) 29-05-45
Copenhagen, Denmark—Govinda's, Soldalen 21, 2100 Copenhagen / (1) 18-43-78
Gothenburg, Sweden—Paradisvagen 11, 43331 Partille / (31) 44-46-36
Grodinge, Sweden—Korsnas Gard, 140 32 / (753) 291-51
Helsinki, Finland—Govinda's, Jaakarinkatu 10D, Helsinki 15 / (65) 0039
Heidelberg, W. Germany—Kurfursten Anlage 5, 6900 Heidelberg / (6221) 15-101
Madrid, Spain—Calle del Tutor No. 27, Madrid 8 / (9) 1-247-6667
Paris, France—Chateau d'Ermenonville, 60440 Nanteuil le Haudouin 68950 / (4) 454-0400
Septon, Belgium—Chateau-de Petit Somme, Septon 5482 / (86) 322-480
Stockholm, Sweden—Fridhemsgatan 22, 112 40 Stockholm / (8) 549-002
Vienna, Austria—Center for Vedic Studies, Am Lugeck 1-2, 1010 Wien / (222) 52-98-25
Zurich, Switzerland—Bergstrasse 54, 8032 Zurich / (1) 69-33-88
FARMS
Almviks Gard, Sweden—15300 Jarna / (755) 52068
Bavarian Forest (Bayrischer Wald), W. Germany (Nava-Jiyāḍa-Nṛsiṁha-Kṣetra)—(contact ISKCON Heidelberg)

158

Brihuega, Spain (New Vraja Mandala)—(Santa Clara) Brihuega, Guadalajara / (11) 280-018
Dudingen, Switzerland—Im Stillen Tal, CH3186 Dudingen (FR) / (37) 43-26-98
Lugano, Switzerland—The Gokula Project, La Pampa, 6981 Sessa (Malcantone) TI / (91) 73-25-73
Valencay, France (New Māyāpur)—Lucay-Le-Male, 36 600 / (54) 40-26-88
   RESTAURANTS
Paris—L'arbre a Soubaits, 15 Rue du Jour, 75001 / 233-2769

AUSTRALASIA
AUSTRALIA
Adelaide—69 Belair Rd., Kingswood (mail: P.O. Box 235, Kingswood, SA 5062) / (8) 272-0488
Brisbane—95 Bank Road, Graceville (mail: P.O. Box 649, Toowong, QLD 4066) / (7) 379-5008
Cairns—69 Spence St. (mail: P.O. Box 5238, Cairns Mail Centre, QLD 4870) / (70) 51-8601
Canberra—59 Argyle Sq. (cnr. Ainsley Ave. & Kogarah Lane), Reid (Mail: P.O. Box 567, Civic
   Square, Canberra, ACT 2608) / (62) 48-9620
Hobart—63 King St., Sandy Bay (mail: P.O. Box 579, Sandy Bay, Tas. 7005) / (2) 23-4569
Melbourne—197 Danks St., Albert Park, VIC 3205 (mail: P.O. Box 125) / (3) 699-5122
Perth—590 William St., Mt. Lawley, WA 6050 (mail: P.O. Box 598, West Perth, WA 6005) / (9)
   328-9171
Surfer's Paradise—2804 Gold Coast Highway, QLD 4217 / (75) 38-5060
Sydney—112 Darlinghurst Rd., King's Cross (mail: P.O. Box 159, King's Cross, NSW 2011) / (2)
   357-5162
   FARMS
Colo (Bhaktivedanta Ashram)—Upper Colo Rd., Central Colo (mail: P.O. Box 493, St. Mary's,
   NSW 2760) / (45) 75-5284
Murwillumbah (New Govardhana)—'Eungella,' Tyalgum Rd. via Murwillumbah (mail: P.O. Box
   687, NSW 2484) / (66) 72-1903
Riverina (New Gaudadesh)—Old Renmark Rd., via Wentworth, NSW 2648 (mail: P.O. 2446,
   Mildura, VIC 3500) / (50) 27-8226
   RESTAURANTS
Adelaide—Govinda's (at ISKCON Adelaide)
Cairns—Gopal's (at ISKCON Cairns)
Melbourne—Gopal's, 139 Swanston St. / (3) 63-1578
Melbourne—Gopal's, Crossways, 1st Fl., 11–15 Elizabeth St. / (3) 62-2800
Surfer's Paradise—Gopal's, 2995 Gold Coast Hwy., QLD 4217 / (75) 38-5060
Sydney—Gopal's, 18A Darcy St., Parramatta / (2) 635-0638
Sydney—Govinda's and Govinda's Take-away (both at ISKCON Sydney)
Sydney—Hare Kṛṣṇa Free Food Centre, Victoria St., King's Cross
   NEW ZEALAND AND FIJI
Auckland, New Zealand—Hwy. 18, Riverhead (next to Huapai Golf Course) (Mail: R.D. 2,
   Kumeu) / 412-8075
Christchurch, New Zealand—83 Bealey Ave. (mail: P.O. Box 2298) / 6-1965
Lautoka, Fiji—5 Tavewa Ave. (mail: P.O. Box 125) / 61-633, ext. 48
Suva, Fiji—P.O. Box 6376, Nasinu / 391-282
Wellington, New Zealand—9 Shalimar Crescent, Khandallah, Wellington (mail: P.O. Box 2753) /
   79-6157
   RESTAURANT
Auckland—Gopal's, 1st Fl., Civic House, 291 Queen St. / 3-4885

LATIN AMERICA
BRAZIL
Belem, PA—Av. Gentil Bitencourt, passagem Mac Dowell, 96 (entre Dr. Morais e Benjamin
   Constant)
Belo Horizonte, MG—Av. Getulio Vargas, 167, Funcionarios / 223-2776
Brazilia, DF—MSPW Quadra 13, conj. 6, Casa 8 / 553-1173
Campo Grande, MS—Av. Julio de Castilhos, 1762, Santo Amaro
Curtiba, PR—Av. Sete de Setembro, 1594, Alto da Rua Quinze
Florianopolis, SC—Rua Ivo Reis Montenegro, 421, Itaguacu
Fortaleza, CE—Rua Jose Lourenco, 2114, Aldeota
Manaus, AM—Rua Leopoldo Neves, 387, B Sao Raimundo
Porto Alegre, RS—Rua Tomas Flores, 327, Bonfim / 27-3078
Recife, PE—Rua Parnamirim, 329, Parnamirim / (1) 268-1908
Ribeirao Preto, SP—Rua Campos Sales, 542, Centro
Rio de Janeiro, RJ—Ladeira da Gloria, 98, Gloria / 285-5643
Salvador, BA—Rua Alvaro Adorno 17, Brotas, 40.000 / (71) 244-1072
Santos, SP—C. P. 2125, Gonzaga
Sao Luiz, MA—Av. Casemiro Junior, 564, Anil
Sao Paulo, SP—Rua Bom Pastor, 798, Ipiranga (mail: C. p. 4855-01000) / (11) 63-1674
Sao Paulo, SP—Rua Paraiso, 642, Paraiso
Teresopolis, RJ—Vrajabhumi / 742-3011
Vitoria, ES—Rua Cesar Helal, 288, Bento Ferreira

FARM

Pindamonhangaba, SP (New Gokula)—Riberao Grande (mail: C.P. 108, 12.400 Pinda)

MEXICO

Guadalajara—Morelos No. 1514 Sector Hildago, Jalisco / 26-12-78

Mexico City—Gob. Tiburcio Montiel 45, San Miguel Chapultepec, D.F. 18 / (905) 271-0132

Mexico City—Govinda's Cultural Center, Insurgentes Sur 2384-1, 01000 D.F. / 548-9323

Monterrey—General Albino Espinoza, 345 Pte., Zona Centro, Monterrey, N.L. / 42-67-66

Morelia—Ticateme No. 52 pte., Col. Selix Ireta 58070

Puebla—Rio Nazos 5016, Col. Jardines San Miguel / 45-90-47

Vera Cruz—Calle 3, Carebelas No. 784, Fraccionamienito Reforma / 50759

FARM

Tulancingo, Hidalgo (Nueva Gauḍa-Maṇḍala-Bhūmi)—(contact ISKCON Mexico City)

PERU

Arequipa—Jerusalem 402 / 229-523

Cuzco—Calle Plaza San Francisco No. 360 (altos)

Chosica—Jr. Chile 136

Huancayo—Av. Giraldez 652

Lima—Avenida San Martin 135 / 670-405

Miraflores—Av. Schell 630 / 442-505

Trujillo—Jr. Bolivar 768

FARM COMMUNITY

Gauranga Sevak—Bellavista, Hvallaga, San Martin

RESTAURANTS

Arequipa—(at ISKCON Arequipa)

Barranco—Av. Grav 137

Cuzco—Calle Espaderos 128 (near Plaza de Armas)

Lima—Jr. Azangaro 149

Miraflores—(at ISKCON Miraflores)

OTHER COUNTRIES

Buenos Aires, Argentina—Centro Bhaktivedanta, Andonaegui 2054, (1431) Buenos Aries

Cali, Colombia—Avenida 9 Norte, 17-33 / 621-688

Caracas, Venezuela—Calle Luis Roche 61, Colinas de Los Chaguaramos / 751-3026

Cochabamba, Bolivia—P.O. Box 3988 / 46441

Concepcion, Chile—Nongue, 588 / 23150

Cordoba, Argentina—Ramirez de Arellano 680, (5000) Alta Cordoba

Crabwood Creek, Guyana—Grant 1803, Sec. D, Corentyne, Berbice

Georgetown, Guyana—24 Uitvlugt Front, West Coast Demerara

Guayaquil, Ecuador—V. E. Estrada 110, Circunvalacion Norte / 382-439

La Paz, Bolivia—Avenida Herando Siles 6239 (mail: Casilla 10278 Obrajes) / 785-023

Medellin, Colombia—Calle 56 (Bolivia), Parque de Bolivar

Montevideo, Uruguay—Casilla 10,531, Suc. Pluna

Panama, Republic of Panama—Via las Cumbres, entrada a Villa Zaita, frente a INPSA No. 10 (mail: P.O. Box 6-29-54) / 681-070

Quito, Ecuador—Carron 641 Amazones / 520-466

San Jose, Costa Rica—100 mtrs. sureste de aptos Torre Blanca Urbanizacion Carmiol, Montes de Oca, Casa No. 49 (mail: P.O. Box 166, Paseo Estudiantes, Z-1002)

San Salvador, El Salvador—67 Avenida Sur No. 15, Colonia Escalon

Santiago, Chile—Estudiantes 150

Santo Domingo, Dominican Republic—Calle Cayetano Rodriguez No. 254 / (809) 688-7242

Trinidad and Tobago, West Indies—Prabhupada Ave., Longdenville, Chaguanas

FARMS

Guayaquil (Nuevo Nilācala)—(contact ISKCON Guayaquil)

Guyana—Seawell Village, Corentyne, East Berbice

San Salvador, El Salvador—Carretera a Santa Ana, Km. 34, Canton Los Indios, Zapotitan, Dpto. de La Libertad

RESTAURANTS

Buenos Aires, Argentina—Madre Tierra, Mendoza 2320, (1428) Buenos Aries

Guayaquil, Ecuador—Govinda's (at ISKCON Guayaquil)

Quito—Govinda's, Esmeracoas 853 y Venezuela / 511-083

San Jose—50 metros al este de la casa amarilla, Avenida 7, No. 1325

San Salvador, El Salvador—Govinda's 7a Calle Oriente No. 155 / 218-035

Santiago, Chile—Govinda's (at ISKCON Santiago)

ASIA

INDIA

Ahmedabad, Gujarat—7, Kailas Society, Ashram Rd., 380 009 / 449-935

Bamanbore, Gujarat—N.H. 8-B, Surendranagar (city office: 32 Ananta Nagar, Kalavad Rd., Rajkot 36 003)

Bangalore, Karnataka—34/A, 9th 'B' Cross, West of Chord Rd., Mahalaxmi Layout, 560 086 (mail: P.O. Box 5181) / 80418

Baroda, Gujarat—18 Sujata Society Gotri Rd., 390 015 / 66499
Bhubaneswar, Orissa—National Hwy. No. 5, Nayapali, 751 001 / 53125
Bombay, M.S.—Hare Krishna Land, Juhu 400 054 / 626-860
Calcutta, W. Bengal—3 Albert Rd., 700 017 / 443-757
Chandigarh, Punjab—Hare Krishna Land, Dakshin Marg, Sector 36-B, 160 036 / 26674
Chhaygharia (Haridaspur), W. Bengal—Thakur Haridas Sripatbari Sevashram, P.O. Chhaygharia, P.S. Bongaon, Dist. 24 Pargonas
Gauhati, Assam—P.B. No. 127, 781 001
Hyderabad, A.P.—Hare Krishna Land, Nampally Station Rd., 500 001 / 51018
Imphal, Manipur—Hare Krishna Land, Airport Rd., 795 001
Madras, Tamil Nadu—232 Kilpauk Garden Rd., Madras 600 010 / 662-286
Mayapur, W. Bengal—Shree Mayapur Chandrodaya Mandir, P.O. Shree Mayapur Dham (Dist. Nadia)
New Delhi—M-119 Greater Kailash 1, 110 048 / 642058
Pandharpur, M.S.—Hare Krishna Ashram, across Chandrabhaga River, Dist. Sholapur, 413 304
Pune, Maharashtra—4 Tarapoor Rd.
Silchar, Assam—Mahaprabhu Colony, Malugram, Cachar District, 788 002
Surat, Gujarat—Rander Rd., Jahangirpura, Surat, 395 005 / 84215
Tirupati, A.P.—No. 37, B Type, T. T. D. Qrs., Vinayaka Nagar, K. T. Rd., 517 501 / 2285
Trivandrum, Kerala—TC224/1485, W/C Hospital Rd., Thychaud, 695 014 / 68197
Vrindavan, U.P.—Krishna-Balaram Mandir, Bhaktivedanta Swami Marg, Raman Reti, Mathura / 178
FARMS
Hyderabad—P.O. Dabilpur Village, Medchal Taluc, Hyderabad District, 501 401
Mayapur—(contact ISKCON Mayapur)
RESTAURANTS
Bombay—Govinda's (at Hare Krishna Land)
Vrindavan—Krishna-Balaram Mandir Guesthouse
OTHER COUNTRIES
Bali, Indonesia—Jalan Sagamona 17, Renon, Denpasar
Bangkok, Thailand—139, Soi Puttha-Osoth, New Road / 233-2488
Hong Kong—5 Homantin St., Flat 23, Kowloon / (3) 7122-630
Jakarta, Indonesia—Jalan Kamboja 10 & 12, Tomang Raya / 599-301
Kathmandu, Nepal—Sri Kunj, Kamaladi
Kuala Lumpur, Malaysia—Lot. 23 Jalan 18 22, Taman Kanagapuram, Petaling Jaya
Manila, Phillipines—41 Guevarra St., San Francisco—Delmonte, Quezon City, P.I. / 971-760
Taipei, Taiwan—(mail; c/o ISKCON Hong Kong)
Tel Aviv, Israel—P.O. Box 48163, Tel Aviv 61480
Tokyo, Japan—2-41-12 Izumi, Suginami-ku, Tokyo T168 / (3) 327-1541
FARM
Cebu, Phillipines (Hare Kṛṣṇa Paradise)—231 Pasabungan Rd., Basak, Mandaue / 83254
RESTAURANT
Cebu, Phillipines—Govinda's, 26 Sanchiangko St.

AFRICA
Abeokuta, Nigeria—behind NET, Ibadan Rd. (mail: P.O. Box 5177, Abeokuta, Ogun State)
Accra, Ghana—582 Blk. 20, Odokor, Official Town (mail: P.O. Box 01568, Osu)
Benin City, Nigeria—22 Akele Dr. (off Upper Mission Rd.), New Benin, Benin City (mail: P.O. Box 3681, Benin City, Bendel State, Nigeria)
Buea, Cameroon—Southwest Province (mail: c/o Yuh Laban Nkesah, P and T, VHS)
Durban (Natal), S. Africa—P.O. Box 212, Cato Ridge, Natal 3680 / (325) 219-19
Ibadan, Nigeria—P.O. Box 9996 U.I.
Kitwe, Zambia—P.O. Box 20242
Lagos, Nigeria—No. 2 Murtala Mohammed International Airport Expressway, Mafaluku (mail: P.O. Box 8793, Lagos)
Mauritius—White House, Celicourt Antelme St., Quartre Bornes (mail: P.O. Box 108, Quartre Bornes, Mauritius 46804)
Mombasa, Kenya—Madhvani House, Sauti Ya Kenya and Kisumu Rds. (mail: P.O. Box 82224, Mombasa) / 312-248
Nairobi, Kenya—Muharoni Close, off West Nagara Rd. (mail: P.O. Box 28946, Nairobi) / 744-365
Nkawkaw, Ghana—P.O. Box 329, Nkawkaw
Port Harcourt, Nigeria—2 Eligbam Rd., (cnr. Eligbam and Obana Obhan St.), G.R.A. II (mail: P.O. Box 4429, Trans Amadi)
Takoradi, Ghana—64 Windy Ridge (mail: P.O. Box 328)
FARM
Mauritius (ISKCON Vedic Farm)—Beau Bois, Bon Acceuil

Books by His Divine Grace A.C. Bhaktivedanta Swami Prabhupāda

Bhagavad-gītā As It Is
Śrīmad-Bhāgavatam, cantos 1–10 (30 vols.)
Kṛṣṇa, the Supreme Personality of Godhead (3 vols.)
Śrī Caitanya-caritāmṛta (17 vols.)
Teachings of Lord Caitanya
The Nectar of Devotion
The Nectar of Instruction
Śrī Īśopaniṣad
Easy Journey to Other Planets
Kṛṣṇa Consciousness: The Topmost Yoga System
Perfect Questions, Perfect Answers
Dialectical Spiritualism—A Vedic View of Western Philosophy
Teachings of Lord Kapila, the Son of Devahūti
Transcendental Teachings of Prahlād Mahārāja
Teachings of Queen Kuntī
Kṛṣṇa, the Reservoir of Pleasure
The Science of Self-Realization
The Path of Perfection
Light of the Bhāgavata
Life Comes From Life
The Perfection of Yoga
Beyond Birth and Death
On the Way to Kṛṣṇa
Geetār-gān (Bengali)
Vairāgya-vidyā (Bengali)
Buddhi-yoga (Bengali)
Bhakti-ratna-bolī (Bengali)
Rāja-vidyā: The King of Knowledge
Elevation to Kṛṣṇa Consciousness
Kṛṣṇa Consciousness: The Matchless Gift
Back to Godhead magazine (founder)

*A complete catalog is available upon request. For your free copy,
call toll free (800) 356-3000 or write to the address below.*

Bhaktivedanta Book Trust
3764 Watseka Avenue
Los Angeles, CA 90034

YES!

Please send my free copy of (choose one): ☐ *Coming Back* ☐ *Chant and Be Happy.* I'm enclosing $1 to cover postage and handling.

☐ Please also send your free mail order catalog.

Name _____

Address _____

City _____ State _____ ZIP _____

(Offer good in USA only)

Send to: **Bhaktivedanta Book Trust, 3764 Watseka Ave.,
Los Angeles, CA 90034**